YOUR
MONEY
OR
YOUR
LIFE

YOUR
MONEY
OR
YOUR
LIFE

The Health Care Crisis Explained

Marc J. Roberts, Ph.D.
WITH
Alexandra T. Clyde

MAIN
STREET
BOOKS

DOUBLEDAY
New York   London   Toronto   Sydney   Auckland

A MAIN STREET BOOK

PUBLISHED BY DOUBLEDAY

a division of Bantam Doubleday Dell Publishing Group, Inc.
1540 Broadway, New York, New York 10036

MAIN STREET BOOKS, DOUBLEDAY, and the portrayal of a building with a
tree are trademarks of Doubleday, a division of Bantam Doubleday Dell
Publishing Group, Inc.

Design: Stanley S. Drate/Folio Graphics Co. Inc.

Library of Congress Cataloging-in-Publication Data
Roberts, Marc J.
Your money or your life : the health care crisis explained / Marc J. Roberts
with Alexandra T. Clyde.—1st ed.
p. cm.
Includes bibliographical references.
1. Medical care—United States. 2. Insurance, Health—United
States. 3. Medical care. Cost of—United States. I. Clyde,
Alexandra T. II. Title.
RA395.A3R58 1994
362.1′0973—dc20 93-35724
CIP

ISBN 0-385-47356-7

1 3 5 7 9 10 8 6 4 2

First Edition

For Howard H. Hiatt
former Dean of the Harvard School
of Public Health
friend, mentor, teacher, leader

CONTENTS

THE CRISIS RECOGNIZED

Why Now?

On the screen was the dramatic image of a jailhouse door closing behind a disheveled individual. The voice-over narration intoned, "If people have a fundamental right to a lawyer when they are accused of a crime, working people should have a right to a doctor when they get sick." That campaign commercial, with its call for national health insurance, helped produce the stunning victory of Harris Wofford in Pennsylvania's special U.S. Senate race in 1991. Wofford, in turn, sent a powerful message to those preparing for the 1992 elections. For the first time, health care had played a decisive role in a major election.

In early 1991, only 1 percent of the public felt that health care was the nation's most important problem. Less than a year later, Democrats and Republicans alike ranked it as the second most important issue, after the overall economy, in the presidential and congressional elections. And for Bill Clinton, reforming the nation's health care system became both a major campaign theme and a top priority for the new administration he led into Washington in January of 1993.

All this has been quite surprising to the small group of academics, think-tank scholars, government analysts, and private consultants who comprise the nation's loose-knit community of health policy experts. Whenever there is a conference on health care, the invitation list tends to follow the *Casablanca* principle. The relevant line is spoken by Claude Rains, playing the French policeman, near the end of that movie. "Major Strasser's been shot," he says. "Round up the usual suspects." Accepted wisdom among these "suspects" was that no fundamental changes would be made in U.S. health care arrangements beyond the Medicare and Medicaid programs initiated in 1966. Over the years, various proposals had been introduced in Congress, yet none received serious consideration. Now suddenly it has become almost impossible to open a newspaper or a magazine without encountering an analysis of the health care crisis, and another proposal for health care reform.

Television, too, has done its part. Repeatedly we have seen these same "usual suspects" holding forth, or witnessed painful interviews with families bankrupted by their inadequate insurance, or heard from doctors upset at increasing paperwork. Yet for all this media attention, the actual dimensions of the health care crisis, and the alternatives for dealing with it, remain fearsomely obscure. Terms and jargon proliferate: HMO, PPO, managed care, managed competition, single-payer, risk adjustment, risk management, etc., etc. How is anyone who is not one of the "usual suspects" to understand all this? What are the issues and choices actually facing the nation as the policy debate reaches its expected crescendo of both obscurity and acrimony in the months to come?

The goal of this book is to provide an outsider's guide both to the health care system and to the various reform options that might be chosen in either the current round, or in future rounds, of health care policy-making. For still more health care reform almost certainly lies in the nation's future. The reason is simple if sobering: there just is no way to give Americans everything they want from their health care system. What we apparently desire is unlimited access to the world's best care, with no organizational or bureaucratic barriers, and without imposing real costs on either ourselves, our government, or the economy.

Such a promised land is not attainable. Any system will cost more, have less perfect access, and be more bureaucratic than most of us would like. The question is, why is this so, and how can we proceed to at least do the best we can? For while no nation's system is perfect, the citizens (and doctors) of some other countries (e.g., Canada and Germany) do tend to be more satisfied with their health care than their counterparts in the United States. This suggests the happy thought that some progress should be possible.

As the nation pursues health care reform, it will confront a deep dilemma. On one hand, the structure of the system is so complex and resilient that minor changes in public policy will not produce major improvements in performance. On the other hand, really significant change will not come easily, since those who benefit from the status quo will vigorously oppose any reform that does not protect their interests.

Moreover, the health care system is deeply interwoven into the fabric of American life. It reflects many of our essential social and economic attitudes. Thus, throughout the reform effort important values like equity, efficiency, and fairness will be at stake. How America deals with the current health care crisis will say a great deal about both our national character and the character of our political institutions.

But first, why all the uproar? Why have I written, and why are you taking the time to read, this book?

The Increasingly Worried Middle Class

While it may not reflect well on our national generosity, health care reform has *not* risen to the top of our national agenda out of an altruistic concern for the uninsured or because low-income individuals have relatively poor access to care. Those Americans with adequate health insurance have been perfectly willing merely to bemoan the fate of the least well off, while doing little to correct it, for the last twenty-five years.

Then why the sudden surge of interest in health care reform? The answer is that the problems of the health care system are increasingly affecting middle-class Americans. Sharply rising health care costs and insecurity about future insurance coverage are no longer just the concerns of the uninsured and those with low incomes.

While 35 million Americans lack health insurance at any point in time, closer to 63 million will be uninsured at some point over the next two years. This is because many people move into and out of uninsured status as they lose or change jobs. There are also those who worry they might lose their health insurance as a result of economic hard times, those who feel they can't change jobs because they might lose their coverage, and those who have a family member or relative who is sick and cannot obtain affordable insurance. Then there are those who believe their insurance costs too much and covers too little, as well as those who already depend on publicly financed coverage. In sum, health insurance is a personally important issue to perhaps 50 percent, rather than 15 percent, of the population. That is a big number in a society in which only 60 percent of the people vote—big enough to get the attention of any politician.

At the same time, during the 1980s, the nation's middle class saw its real income decline and its share of the total tax burden increase. The poor performance of the U.S. economy has also produced a general sense of economic insecurity. The signs are all around us: wave after wave of corporate downsizing, young couples unable to afford new homes, and families discovering that a second income is a necessity to preserve their living standards. More and more Americans are feeling the concern that led to some famous advice from the great relief pitcher Satchel Paige. Paige, of advanced but indeterminate age, once spoke about his philosophy of life. "Don't look back," he said. "Something might be gaining on you."

It was exactly Wofford's ability to focus this generalized unease on health care that helped define the shape and success of his campaign. He articulated the middle class's distress at suffering from a "double whammy" of exploding health care costs and decreasing coverage.

The concern of working Americans about losing their coverage is not unfounded. As Henry Kissinger once said, "Just because you are paranoid does not mean they are not out to get you." Health insurance coverage actually declined in all income groups *except* the poor between 1988 and 1991. As a result, 86 percent of the uninsured are members of working households.

There are two underlying structural forces behind these trends. First, a growing share of all employment is in the service and small business sectors, where employer-sponsored insurance is less common. Manufacturing jobs, which traditionally have offered extensive health insurance, have actually been declining. Second, as the cost of health insurance has gone up, employers have increasingly tried to shift some of these costs to their employees—making them pay higher premiums, or pay more for care when they do use the system. Combined with lower real incomes, increased cost sharing has led to an increase in the share of personal expenditures that citizens now devote to medical care. And rising insurance rates have made health coverage unaffordable for many low-wage workers. Americans now understand—all too well—the perilous link between having health insurance and holding the right kind of job. Yet, when do the risks of financial devastation from a major illness make health insurance particularly vital? The answer is, when someone's economic prospects are uncertain because they don't have a job!

Americans are also upset because they are encountering increasing constraints on their free choice of providers—doctors and hospitals. To contain costs, health insurance plans now frequently limit employees to certain physicians and hospitals that agree to cooperate with cost-control efforts. Today, more than half of all those in employer-based health plans are in such "managed care" plans. These seek to control costs by aggressively pushing providers to justify their use of tests, treatments, and hospital admissions.

In addition, Americans who are ill, or who have a history of serious medical problems, have discovered that changing jobs might cost them their insurance for precisely the condition from which they are suffering. Insurers call this a "preexisting condition" exclusion. Currently, one in twenty Americans has a health insurance policy which, due to such an exclusion, does not cover the illness he or she most needs it for. Close to one third of the population has or has had an illness that could affect their future insurability under the current system. As a result of these worries, one in four American families has a member who cannot change jobs because their health benefits are not portable—a phenomenon termed "job-lock."

The elderly—whose political power is legendary—are also feeling the pinch. Even with Medicare, the elderly pay a substantial fraction of their health care costs with their own resources. Supplemental insurance, which many rely on to cover this "gap," is becoming prohibitively expensive, especially for those on fixed incomes. At the same time businesses are also trying to minimize the coverage they offer their retirees.

Many of these forces are reflected in the following true story about an upper-middle-class insurance executive who lost his job in a 1992 managerial downsizing. He had trouble finding comparable work and decided to use his contacts to do some private consulting. He continued his family health insurance through his old employer—which he was legally entitled to do for two years under the provisions of a federal law called COBRA (the Consolidated Omnibus Budget Reconciliation Act of 1985).

In 1993, his wife discovered that she had cancer. Our subject realized that there was only one more year of COBRA coverage. Other nongroup plans were not likely to cover immediately the costs of treating his wife's cancer because they excluded preexisting conditions. He then learned that Blue Cross-Blue Shield, in the state where he lived, was about to offer a new community-rated health insurance plan for individuals ("community-rated" plans charge everyone more or less the same regardless of health status). The preexisting condition exclusion for this plan lasted only twelve months. Desperate, if grateful, for the new option, he decided to pay the very high cost of *two* insurance policies for almost a whole year until his COBRA policy ran out. This still left his wife uncovered for two months between the end of their COBRA policy and the end of the preexisting condition exclusion under the new plan. But that was better than having her condition uncovered for twelve months.

This individual has been a Republican all of his life and was disappointed with the election of Bill Clinton, whom he viewed as just another "tax and spend liberal." But now he expresses great respect for Clinton's efforts to deal with health care reform. "At least he's trying to do something," he says. Ironically, the absurdity of the current system became clear to him only when personal experience provided an insight that thirty years in the insurance business had never offered.

This story illustrates many of the opportunities and difficulties that confront health care reformers. There is a desire for a more rational, universal system and a growing sense of personal anxiety about existing insurance. Polls, however, reveal that many Americans are not willing to spend a great deal more to finance such a system. Perhaps this is because they generally believe that a grab bag of nonsystemic forces accounts for health care cost increases: drug company profits; malpractice litigation; doctors' incomes; fraud, waste, and abuse in government programs.

The truth is that improving the coverage of most Americans, and also covering the uninsured, will increase health care costs. And it will take many years and great effort to transform our current system sufficiently to control the powerful pressures for continuing cost increases. Putting this puzzle together in a program that can actually pass Congress will be an enormous challenge, especially with the heightened antitax feeling left by the 1993 budget debate.

Business Begins to Move

The last great health insurance reform in the United States, the passage of Medicare and Medicaid, came after twenty years of uninterrupted economic growth. The United States was one of the few major industrial nations whose economy was intact after World War II. As a result, we were in an ideal position to supply the rest of the world with the equipment, machinery, and technology it needed to rebuild. The growth that was fueled by this position helped produce an enormous sense of prosperity and possibility. Expanding health insurance for low-income individuals and the elderly seemed a matter of simple decency that a prosperous nation could easily afford. After all, health care was only 6 percent of the GNP in 1965, less than half its current share!

What has happened to the U.S. economy since? Those former markets, whose industrial structures lay in ruins, are now our competitors. England, Germany, Japan, France, and Italy, not to mention Taiwan, Korea, India, and Brazil, are all competing in the world's markets, trying to sell what we sell. And in dealing with that competition, the United States is handicapped by its need to cope with many profound social problems like crime, drugs, poor schools, and growing family disorganization. All of these diminish the quality of the work force, place demands on our educational system, draw off resources into other government programs, and limit our capacity to produce efficiently. Moreover, these difficulties are not going to be overcome easily or quickly.

These strained competitive circumstances have led more and more companies to support health care reform. In an increasing number of cities, local business coalitions have been established to encourage health care cost containment. And business support has been critical to several state efforts at health care reform. At the same time, however, business has seldom played an aggressive leadership role. What accounts for this dual picture of widespread, yet modest, efforts?

International competitiveness admittedly depends on many factors, including worker productivity relative to worker compensation, materials prices, the sophistication of factory equipment, and so on. Of all of these, health care costs often seem relatively identifiable and potentially controllable. For the fact is that U.S. per capita health care costs are 50 to 100 percent above those of most other industrialized nations. Moreover, many foreign firms contribute much less—or even nothing—to their employees' health care costs. Auto executives recently pointed out that even if American automobile manufacturers were as technologically efficient as the Japanese, they probably could not overcome the 750-dollars-a-car difference in health care costs between the two countries. That amount, by the way, is greater than the manufacturer's profit margin on most vehicles.

Even for companies that don't compete internationally, health insurance costs have become increasingly burdensome. Corporate spending on health care increased from 28 to 56 percent of pretax profits between 1980 and 1989. Many plans now cost companies $5,000 per worker per year, compared to less than $1,000 ten years ago. Moreover, the need to manage these costs imposes substantial managerial burdens and administrative costs on companies. And the unpredictability of next year's premium increases can add significant uncertainty to overall business financial planning.

Trying to control health care costs can also produce unhappy employees, especially when companies try to shift costs back to workers. When a strong union is trying to protect a generous benefit package, built up over twenty-five years of hard bargaining, the conflict can reach epic proportions. Indeed disagreements over health care costs are now one of the leading sources of labor disputes in the United States, accounting for fully one third of all strikes in recent years.

Small business has been especially hard hit. While many small employers would like to provide insurance, they face increasing rates for, and sometimes even flat-out denials of, coverage by insurers. All of this has resulted in an actual decline in the extent to which they offer insurance coverage. From 1989 to 1991, the percentage of firms employing twenty-five or fewer workers that provided coverage fell from 39 percent to 32 percent; for firms with twenty-five to ninety-nine workers, the decline was from 93 percent to 81 percent.

There are several reasons small businesses have particular trouble, as we explore in more detail in Chapter 3. Because administrative costs increase rapidly as firm size declines, they pay more for the same insurance coverage. (The fees charged by insurers are 40 percent of premiums for small groups, compared to 5.5 percent for the largest companies, with the overall average about 14 percent.) Small businesses also have less market power when it comes to negotiating with providers, and less experience when it comes to buying insurance and controlling its cost. Moreover, small employers with a few sick or high-risk employees can find that insurance has become unaffordable or even unattainable, because they cannot spread the costs of caring for these individuals over a large employee pool.

Why then has business activism remained so moderate? Why aren't business executives storming Congress and the White House demanding reform, especially since employers who do provide coverage wind up cross-subsidizing the care of the uninsured? In part the answer is that the diverse interests of the business community leave it divided over the specifics of any plan. Under our currently fragmented system, large employers have the power to negotiate with providers for discounted prices. They have the expertise to flexibly manage their health care benefits to suit their specific circumstance. And they can save money by self-insuring.

As a result, in 1991 employers with over 1,000 employees saw the cost of their traditional medical plans rise only 9.6 percent, compared to an average cost increase of 17.3 percent for all employers. Some or all of these advantages might vanish with universal coverage if, for example, rates and benefits were standardized.

Not even all large employers share the same perspectives. Industrial firms with strong unions often feel locked into traditional "Cadillac" benefit plans that provide relatively extensive coverage and free choice of provider. Such employers are likely to feel that their fate is tied to the rate of cost increase in the health care system as a whole, since there is little they can do to influence their workers' utilization. On the other hand, high-tech companies with white-collar work forces are more likely to be well down the road to "managed care," and to believe that they control their costs on their own.

Similarly, there are perfectly good reasons why not all small businesses are actively supporting health care reform. Some fear that universal coverage would involve a government mandate on employers to provide insurance. This might remove their current ability to operate with lower labor costs than their larger competitors. The alternative, a government-financed plan, is often unacceptable to groups committed to less government and lower taxes on general principles.

Small (and large) businesses also have a great deal else to worry about besides health care costs. Their executives have to be concerned primarily with operating their actual businesses. And even in the public policy realm, health care must compete for managerial attention with environmental issues, occupational health and safety, minimum wage, workmen's compensation, tax policy, infrastructure, and a host of other concerns.

Many businesses make money from health care, which further confuses their incentives. General Electric, for example, has a large labor force and pays a great deal for extensive health care benefits. But as one of the nation's leading suppliers of X-ray machines and other high-tech equipment, it probably has mixed feelings about health care cost containment.

But if business has not been the engine driving health care reform—where has the impetus been coming from?

Government Begins to Panic

Of all payers for health care, government itself has the largest interest in controlling costs. Health care spending (over $200 billion on Medicaid and Medicare in 1992) is the fastest-growing part of the federal budget and has emerged as *the* largest obstacle to deficit reduction. In addition, Medicaid expenditures average 14 percent of total state expenditures and have been increasing faster than almost every other component of state budgets. Indeed this year, for the first time, health care will surpass education as the sector that takes the biggest share of total state spending. The inevitable "crowding out" of other programs is a serious problem for many states.

As a result, many in government would now say that the "Titanic" principle applies to health care reform. "If everyone around you is losing their head, while you remain calm, maybe you just don't understand the situation." Health care costs have finally caught the attention of many governors and state legislators.

Of course, not all of these problems are simply due to health cost inflation. The aging of the population means that there are more elderly to enroll in Medicare. Medicaid too has grown, due to liberalized eligibility and an increase in the number of those in poverty. But there have also been major increases in health care costs. These affect not only the cost of public programs but also the substantial expense of insuring public employees.

Public officials feel caught in a fiscal vise. The modest prospects for short-run economic growth imply that tax revenues will grow slowly, while demands for growth-promoting expenditures continue to increase. And in poor times, the demands on social programs also expand.

Solving this dilemma has become more difficult because the public has become increasingly reluctant to support tax increases. Whatever else Ronald Reagan accomplished, he left many Americans very suspicious of any higher taxes on the grounds that their tax money is almost never well spent. Meanwhile, federal budget deficits are already so high that both the public and elected officials are worried that further increases could undermine future prosperity. Indeed interest payments on the federal debt are already squeezing out the dollars available for housing, education, infrastructure, and other national needs.

This dilemma helps explain why major health care initiatives now generally originate from the Executive Branch—whether at the state or federal level. For that is where the trade-offs have to be made among programs. And that is where responsibility rests for politically explosive decisions to increase revenue. It also helps to explain why government's first impulse is often to try to shift costs back to the private sector, thereby only exacerbating the problems of business.

A New Administration Takes the Stage

Many of the "usual suspects" have argued for years that national health care reform would not occur until a president made it a major priority—just as Lyndon Johnson did in 1965. This explains why the election of Bill Clinton produced such a stir. By themselves, the trends that we have reviewed might not have been enough to have put health care reform at center stage had they not also intersected with Clinton's own political strategy and personal interests.

In contrast, most recent presidents and presidential candidates have chosen to steer clear of the complexity and controversy of health care reform. George Bush repeatedly defended the system, portraying himself as its protector and incremental improver. And not so many years ago, the otherwise liberal Democratic candidate Walter Mondale, after being briefed on health care for two hours, allegedly turned to his political aides and said, "Keep me the hell out of this political swamp."

As a governor, Bill Clinton served on the National Governors Association health care committee. A self-confessed "policy wonk," he has long been fascinated by the intricacies of the health care system, impressing even the experts with his command of the nuances of health policy. He understands that controlling health care costs is inextricably linked to any progress on deficit reduction, improving U.S. competitiveness, and facilitating job growth. (Small companies, in which much job growth takes place, are especially troubled by high health insurance costs.) It is not too much to say that the funds for investing in infrastructure, education, and job training are being held hostage to Medicare and Medicaid cost increases.

As a centrist, Clinton has been trying to appeal beyond the traditional Democratic base among the disadvantaged. He is reaching out to the middle class, suburban independents, and blue-collar Reagan Democrats—exactly some of those most concerned with health care. This issue offers him the chance to establish a common cause among these groups and other traditional sources of Democratic support. Also, if Clinton is to win over the 20 percent of the electorate that voted for Ross Perot, he must reduce the deficit and, therefore, control health care inflation. Moreover, as Bill Clinton, Rhodes scholar, surely understands, it is his chance to make a historic contribution.

The Task Ahead

So, even at this very preliminary stage in our discussion, we can begin to see what any new plan will have to achieve if it is to respond to the underlying concerns that lie behind the current drive for health care reform. The first task of any reform effort will be to ensure *effective cost control*. Only cost control will help ease business concerns as well as the state and federal budget problems caused by health care cost increases. Cost control will also address middle-class concerns about keeping down both their taxes and premiums. Attempts by any payer (an insurance company, a government health program, or an individual) to control its own costs—without controlling system costs—are ultimately futile. In the end, someone has to pay for all the costs of the system whether through increases in premiums, taxes, or prices.

The second key characteristic of any reform is whether or not it will achieve *universal coverage*. As long as there is only fragmented coverage, insurers will have an incentive to control their costs by pushing those with high medical costs out of their plans.

Since high-cost individuals are those who are sick, we will be left with the same crazy system we have today; everyone will be at risk of losing their insurance exactly when they need it most. That is what preexisting condition exclusions and coverage terminations are all about. The only way to fully solve this problem for the middle class, as well as to address the problem of the uninsured, is to create a universal system.

Third, will we move to *financing based on ability to pay*? Under our current system the primary barrier to insurance coverage is low income. Many people simply can't afford the costs of adequate insurance. Indeed, when individuals get sick, their incomes decrease, so insurance becomes particularly unaffordable just when it is most needed. Thus, the only way to have universal coverage is to employ a financing scheme in which, to a substantial extent, the better off help pay for the less well off, and the healthy pay for the sick.

Moreover, these goals are linked together. It is unlikely we will be able to maintain universal coverage unless we have cost containment. Otherwise, such coverage will cost too much. On the other hand, universal coverage and a rational financing system would make cost containment easier—because we could at least "get our arms around" all costs at once. And in turn, it will be hard to sell ability-to-pay financing to the middle class unless the volume of funds required is kept to a minimum—and that means cost containment.

There are other issues as well that even this brief review suggests. What about quality of care? What about free choice of providers? What about truly equitable access for the sick and the poor? Clearly, reform is going to be a monumentally complex task—and almost as difficult to evaluate as it will be to achieve. Nor will reform come easily. Providers and patients will protest any decrease in their incomes or in the services they receive. The cutbacks and layoffs associated with the downsizing of any industry are painful—and hospitals are major employers in many areas. The health sector, moreover, represents a formidable set of interest groups. The American Medical Association— an organization legendary for using its influence to oppose change—alone gave $3.2 million to federal political candidates in 1992. And just consider the pressure that can be exerted by nurses, hospitals, the health insurance industry, the drug companies, and so on.

Still, there is a window of opportunity for change. There is some increase in business involvement, more political attention, and a growth in middle-class concern. The question is whether this widespread if somewhat unfocused interest can be mobilized behind a specific reform plan which will in fact produce meaningful improvements.

The great challenge to the President will be in *not* trying to please everyone. He cannot provide universal coverage and keep down taxes without cost containment. In a sense he will have to choose his enemies—the providers or the antitax block in Congress. Any cost-containment effort endorsed by the providers has got to be suspect. Any plan that has support from all sides is likely to be deeply flawed. There will be great temptation to pass a plan that deals with many difficulties by ignoring them, a plan whose inadequacies will become evident only after the next presidential election, because the scheme is phased in so slowly.

More than mere pragmatic problem solving is at stake. There are also real value choices. Do we each want to continue to try to limit our own costs by shifting costs to "the other guy"—for example, by not covering people when they get sick—while deep system flaws remain unaddressed? Remember, each of us is at risk for being that "other guy" at some point in our lives. The issue was eloquently stated by the same Republican insurance executive from New Jersey whose experience I recounted earlier. He put it this way. "Is health care a right or a privilege? We seem to be treating it as if it's a privilege and I don't think that is the kind of society that I want to live in." And that is the question the health care crisis poses to us all. Exactly what kind of society *do* we want to live in?

But before we can look at our options for change, we need to know more about where we are. Why are costs so high, coverage so incomplete, and financing so irrational? Only after we investigate these questions will we be able to appreciate fully the alternatives before us.

2

THE UNDERLYING CAUSES OF THE CURRENT HEALTH CARE CRISIS

The Health Care Swamp

The performance of the U.S. health care system is not the result of the evil behavior of a few. Instead, everyone in the system, doctors and patients, hospitals and insurance companies, business and government, interacts in complex ways with each group adapted to its own particular niche. It is like a great primeval swamp in which the fish eat the bugs, the alligators eat the fish, and the alligators die and provide fertilizer for the trees that shelter them all.

Yet unlike a natural ecosystem, the health care "swamp" is a human creation. The "niches" that exist, and the economic and social anatomy of the "creatures" that inhabit them, are the result of past policies and historical developments. Health care reform can and will alter these relationships. But before exploring how that might happen, we need to understand the system itself. What are the incentives and pressures that shape the way health care is produced and delivered in the United States? What are the principal denizens of the swamp and how do they behave?

This chapter reviews the social and scientific forces that shape the overall environment. The next looks at the system itself—at the form and functioning of the major institutional species and their interrelationships. But first context. How do (1) the nature of medical knowledge, (2) current patterns of disease, (3) social attitudes toward health, (4) medical technology, and (5) the political power of the "medical industrial complex" all serve to define the problems of health care reform? While the system is complex, it is useful to remember one of the maxims of the great Yankee catcher and social philosopher Yogi Berra. "You can observe a lot by just watching."

What Doctors Know

For Americans, physicians are an uneasy combination of scientific expert and secular priest. First, there is the doctor-as-Marcus-Welby archetype: sagely experienced and warmly caring. Then there is the doctor as brilliant techno-wizard equipped with an elaborate panoply of electronic equipment, surgical implants, and powerful medications. The patients of the former are compassionately treated and experience an occasional miracle. The patients of the latter enjoy the terrifying yet gratifying fate of biological reconstruction experienced by television's "Six Million Dollar Man."

In fact, both images contain some truth. In recent years there has been an enormous explosion of medical knowledge, and doctors can call on astonishing devices to perform feats impossible only five or six years ago. A great deal is now known about medical science. But case by case clinical decisions still involve much of the intuition and skill of the Marcus Welby–style practitioner. Doctors themselves are perfectly clear on this point. They constantly reiterate that "clinical medicine is more of an art than a science." What they mean by that is that physicians periodically encounter cases where they do not know exactly what is wrong with a given patient, nor precisely how to help make that patient better. Limited knowledge and substantial uncertainty are pervasive in actual medical practice.

Why should that be so? First, clinical experience can be difficult to interpret. The human body has amazing recuperative powers. Suppose a physician tries a medication on a patient, and it apparently works. Was the medication effective or did the patient just happen to recover anyway, without regard to—or perhaps even despite—the treatment? In the eighteenth century, physicians bled patients with high fevers. Many recovered. As a result physicians became ever more convinced that bleeding was appropriate. Actually it was quite harmful. There are other, more modern, examples. In the 1960s a procedure became widely diffused for "freezing" part of the stomach lining of ulcer patients with alcohol. Only after very careful study—and only after many machines to perform the process were sold by their entrepreneurial inventor—was it revealed that the procedure did more harm than good.

Patients' capacity to be influenced by their own faith in a treatment—the so-called "placebo effect"—also greatly complicates the process of learning from experience. Consider a now-famous study of a surgical procedure (known as mammary artery ligation) designed to ameliorate the pain due to poor blood flow to the heart. The theory was that by tying off the mammary artery, more blood would flow to the heart instead through the adjacent coronary artery, lessening the pain. In an experiment that would violate today's ethical guidelines, a surgical team performed two different operations on matched sets of patients. One set got the operation, the other received a comparable dummy procedure (just an incision). The patients did not know who had gotten which treatment. More than half of those who had the procedure reported significant pain relief—but so did an even higher percentage of those who had the dummy operation! The fact is, the mind is connected to the body, and belief can influence experience.

To counteract such phenomena, researchers conduct careful experiments in which a randomly selected group of patients gets a treatment, and a similar group does not. Where possible, such trials are "double blind" so that neither the patients nor their doctors know who is getting which treatment. But such trials are expensive, difficult to organize, and can take years. Since the effects can be quite small, large samples of patients (in the hundreds) are required. Such studies are regularly done for new drugs—an area where there are FDA requirements to meet and potentially large profits to be made. But only modest efforts have been made to go back and verify the bulk of clinical practice. Instead, that has developed over the years based on much less rigorous research.

Even the best clinical trials can leave many detailed questions unresolved. For example, how should treatment vary for patients of different age, weight, gender, or physical condition? Answering that requires still more elaborate trials, where a whole array of treatment options are evaluated in different groups of patients. The fact that many drugs have not even been tested on women shows how infrequently such comprehensive research is actually undertaken.

As a result of all this, doctors have to use their judgment. Is this case a little different from the typical situation, and if so, how should one proceed? But many cases are special or different in some way or another. And doctors vary in their intuitions. As a result, medical practice can vary substantially, even among adjacent regions in a single state. For example, a study conducted by the RAND Corporation, analyzing 4.4 million Medicare beneficiaries, revealed wide variations in rates for surgery and hospitalization. Patients in areas with the highest rates for a particular procedure were eleven times more likely to have a hip operation, six times more likely to have a knee replaced, three times more likely to have coronary bypass surgery, and five times more likely to have a skin biopsy than those in areas with the lowest rates. The explanation of such differences lies in part in variations in "gut judgment"; in the intuition, experience, and training of the practitioners in one area as opposed to another.

Most doctors now accept that such variations are a sign that some areas have inappropriate care—either too much or too little. Some specialty groups and health care organizations have developed rules (called "protocols") to guide and standardize the treatment of specific conditions. (Some physicians object to such protocols as "cookbook medicine," arguing that they do not leave enough room for individual clinical judgment.) Similarly, in some states, physician organizations have brought together groups of doctors in a given specialty to examine patterns of practice. These groups then work with the physicians from regions with noticeably high rates, in order to bring those rates back into line.

The fact that medical practice is not more standardized has several important implications. First, it is a major contributor to higher costs since, as we will see shortly, all the incentives drive doctors toward doing too much rather than too little. Second, it can obviously lead to inappropriate care. Moreover, it increases the possibility of inequitable treatment for the poor and disadvantaged. It may seem easier not to provide a certain treatment for an uninsured patient if what is appropriate is in fact unclear. Thus, clinical ambiguity will make it both more difficult, and more important, for public regulators and private buyers to ensure appropriate care in any reformed health system.

Is Medical Care Too Successful?

Why do Americans seem to be suffering from *increasing* rates of disability? Has our health care system failed us? Ironically, in many ways the reverse is true. We are suffering from what has been called "the failures of success." For example, better emergency care now keeps more victims of heart attacks alive. But as a result, more individuals living nearly normal lives, who in earlier times would have been dead, now report cardiac disability. The same process is at work when we save very low-birth-weight newborns through ultra-high-technology in neonatal intensive-care units. Many of these recover just fine. But a higher percentage of them than in less troubled groups grow up with significant disabilities.

This increase in disability is also due to changes in the diseases Americans suffer from. A hundred years ago, illness in the United States was similar to current patterns in the Third World. The leading causes of death were infectious diseases—scarlet fever, tuberculosis, smallpox, yellow fever, typhoid, diphtheria, influenza, polio, cholera, and so on. Often these diseases attacked children who were (and are) particularly susceptible.

Today Americans—like those in most industrial nations—suffer from different illnesses. With the very important (and very serious) exception of AIDS, relatively few of us now die of infectious disease. Instead we succumb to heart disease, cancer, strokes, and the results of trauma (the latter includes automobile and other accidents, homicide, and suicide). Together these account for more than 70 percent of all deaths—and infection plays little or no role in any of them. Instead, these are chronic, developmental, and degenerative conditions. Our arteries clog or our skin cells multiply uncontrollably as a result of changes in our bodies due to our cumulative life experiences.

Behavior plays a major part in causing these conditions. Tobacco is the most serious culprit. Considering heart disease, lung cancer, and other conditions, smoking is an important cause of perhaps one fourth to one third of all deaths in the United States. But diet, exercise, stress, drug use, and excess alcohol consumption also play a role, including the latter's contribution to automobile accidents and other trauma. (I say excess alcohol consumption because recent studies suggest that moderate beer and wine drinking increase life expectancy by lowering heart attack risks.)

The causes of disability, and of nonfatal illnesses that diminish the quality of life, reveal a similar pattern. True, "old-fashioned" infectious diseases, like colds and flu, cause minor disability. But chronic conditions like heart disease, lung disease, and kidney and liver failure are all important causes of disability. So too are mental illness, dental problems, and the various complaints of old age. Again, chronic and degenerative conditions, with important behavioral causes, shape our overall health circumstances. And, as we now know all too well, certain behaviors are also critical to the spread of our most serious infectious disease—namely AIDS.

This disease pattern has one overwhelming implication. From a technical, actuarial point of view, health care costs are becoming uninsurable. Insurance is designed to protect individuals against uncertain and unanticipated risks. For example, a group of home owners all pay into a fund from which payment goes to those whose houses burn down unpredictably. But with chronic and degenerative conditions, we know with high probability who will be sick next year—namely those who are already sick! Selling health insurance to such a group is like trying to sell fire insurance in a town where some houses are already on fire.

What premium would we have to charge someone for fire

insurance if his house was already burning? The answer is, the full value of that house—exactly because his expected loss is no longer uncertain. The same is true for health insurance. Suppose we look at individuals' actual health states when we decide on their premiums—a practice called "medical underwriting." (Underwriting is simply a word for the process insurance companies use to set premiums.) Those who are already sick would have to pay the very high premiums that reflected their likely health care costs, premiums they probably would not be able to afford. How the health insurance industry has dealt with this reality is discussed in the next chapter.

Moreover, for chronic and developmental conditions, clinical ambiguity tends to be especially serious. A patient with a bacterial infection clearly can benefit from an antibiotic. But how badly clogged should a patient's arteries be before we use some surgical procedure to improve blood flow? Similarly, in exactly what circumstance should drugs be used to lower blood pressure or cholesterol levels? Unlike the presence or absence of a microorganism, there are few "bright lines" in nature to tell us exactly when to intervene in treating chronic and degenerative conditions. Indeed, in such circumstances the whole notion of what care a patient "needs" can be quite ambiguous. We can do more and get more, or do less and get less, but there is no one level of care the patient "needs."

One way to see this is to consider a simple graphical device called a "payoff function." In Figure 1, the bottom of the graph indicates the amount of money devoted to the care of the patient. The vertical dimension measures the gain to the patient of such treatment. (In reality there is no one unique measure of "gain"— it depends on how we value different kinds of outcomes. Also clinical ambiguity means we often don't know the actual payoff function. But let's ignore all these complexities for now.)

What shape do such payoff functions have? Suppose, as in Figure 1, there is a certain threshold level of expenditure at which we can "cure" a patient—level T in the diagram. Then, in a sense, nature is giving us some guidance about how much to spend. Note the function in question looks like a "step." Some steps may be so broad and shallow—cost so much for so little gain—that we might not want to climb them. But if we do act, it

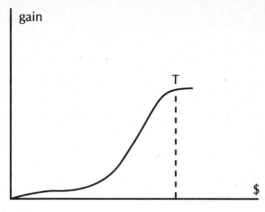

Figure 1

is relatively clear what level of spending makes sense. In such special cases, it is at least meaningful to say that the patient "needs" care at level T.

But these situations are becoming increasingly uncommon. Suppose instead that we confront a situation as in Figure 2, which is more likely to be the case for chronic conditions. Just how far should we go—that is, how much money should we spend? Point X? Y? Z? Notice as we move from X to Y and Y to Z a given added expenditure produces less and less additional gain for the patient. Economists refer to such a pattern as "diminishing marginal returns"—and to medical practice in the region of point Z as "flat of the curve medicine," for obvious reasons.

One characteristic of chronic diseases is that patients tend to deteriorate unless they receive regular care. This helps explain why the sick tend to be poor, and the poor tend to be sick. First the sick have trouble working and tend to be poor. (Thus workers in large companies tend to be healthier than average, which, as we will see, greatly complicates the workings of the health insurance market.) But the causality also runs from poverty to sickness. Poverty is associated with many social problems (e.g., poor nutrition and substance abuse). These tend to make the poor sicker. In addition, as we discuss in Chapter 4, the poor have difficulty in gaining access to the routine ambulatory care that chronic conditions require. Thus they ultimately make greater use

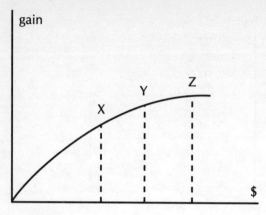

Figure 2

of hospitals than the rich do for those diseases where ambulatory care matters most—often waiting until their condition deteriorates so that they can be admitted.

Note, our experience with infections has influenced our very notion of what a "disease" is. We tend to think of each "disease" as a distinct biological process. Our system of clear and mutually exclusive diagnostic categories reflects this. As long as each illness is caused by a specific micro-organism, this is a sensible approach. A given patient either does or does not have yellow fever or polio (or perhaps in very rare cases, both). Unfortunately, with chronic conditions, the line between "disease" and "nondisease" itself becomes blurred. How high does someone's blood pressure have to go before they have hypertension? If most of us have some obstruction of our coronary arteries, at what point does that become atherosclerosis?

To summarize, Americans now suffer more frequently from chronic and degenerative conditions than from infectious disease. As a result, on an annual basis, many health care costs are now too predictable to be truly insurable, a degree of predictability that will only increase as our knowledge of the genetic basis of disease improves. In addition, deciding just how much to spend on a given case has become increasingly difficult. Indeed the line between who is and is not sick has itself become blurred. This ambiguity leaves room for interested parties to expand the scope of medical practice. It also makes behaviorally oriented prevention much more important. In this context the social problems and lack of ambulatory care experienced by the poor should be of increasing concern, for they help to produce the result that the sick are poorer, and the poor sicker than the middle class.

American Attitudes: Live Free and Don't Die

How did Americans come to view death as optional? We treat it as an unfair way to end the game of life—a field goal scored by the opposition after time has expired. As a result we spend a great deal of our health care dollars on the terminally ill. Compared to other countries, we also do more high-technology lifesaving procedures on the relatively old. In most European countries, for example, kidney transplants beyond age fifty-five or sixty are uncommon.

Why is death so troublesome to Americans? Perhaps it is our social and geographic mobility or a change in our views about religion. Many of us live very different lives from those of our parents, and we live them in different places. As our parents age, guilt and anxiety overwhelm us. We should have visited more often, telephoned more conscientiously. Now we want "everything" to be done. And in the process we fight against our own sense of mortality.

America's romance with technology is also at work. The railroad and repeating firearms won the West—at least in the popular imagination. Interchangeable parts and the assembly line produced the flow of goods that made the U.S.A. the land of opportunity. World War II only solidified this infatuation as technological marvels like radar, sonar, and the atomic bomb advanced the war effort.

After the war, we experienced television and long-playing records, permanent press clothes and nonrusting razor blades, ballpoint pens and automatic transmissions. Again and again, the fabric of our lives, the minute texture of our daily experience, has been altered by science and technology.

Biotechnology has played a large role in this romance. Think about the impact of X-rays and anesthesia. At the time, sulfur drugs and then antibiotics must surely have seemed like "miracle drugs," which is what they were popularly called. If America could build the atom bomb or put a man on the moon (an astonishing achievement in the 1960s) then why couldn't we "cure cancer"? Indeed, that very question was often asked when President Nixon launched his "War on Cancer."

Medicine is not only technology. It is also people. And doctors have their own special place in our social structure. Americans admire talented individuals who succeed in highly competitive environments. Stories of victory through talent and hard work confirm important popular beliefs. For many, "getting into medical school" and "becoming a doctor" were (and are) proof that an individual had both great ability and real self-discipline. The physicians that emerge from such a process—and from the fabled initiation rites of internship and residency—often seem to possess special wisdom. Surely such dedicated individuals, armed with the latest tools of the world's most advanced science can, once again, rise up and block the field goal of impending death!

Ironically, in a world of chronic diseases, the most effective ways to improve health may involve nontechnological approaches like weight loss or smoking cessation. Unfortunately, many of us, when confronted with such situations, still hope that the medical techno-wizards will be able to find a drug or device to save us from the strain and pain of altering our own behavior. (As we explore below, this desire in turn creates incentives for developing new technology that greatly increases medical costs.) Similarly, we increasingly label all social or functional problems as "medical"—thereby allowing us to hope for such scientific salvation. The deterioration of old age is now the province of "gerontology." Alcoholism has become characterized (sociologists would say "socially constructed") as a disease, rather than as a social problem or an individual behavioral failing.

Of course, not all attitudes toward technology and medicine are positive. Environmentalism and the Vietnam War protests reinforced a countercurrent in American society that is skeptical of "establishment" authority and its technology. And some consumer movements in health care—like natural childbirth and holistic medicine—have tapped into that source. So too have efforts to provide patients with more information before they make decisions—as for example a video disk guide to the options for, and consequences of, prostate surgery. But this remains a minor theme in the overall chorus of social approval.

As we contemplate health care reform, we also have to take account of general American views about choice. Many Americans live relatively comfortable lives. Only a declining fraction of us remember rationing during World War II, and as a nation we never experienced the postwar deprivation suffered by Europe or Japan. As a result, middle-class Americans don't expect to have to wait in line. The citizens of other nations may "queue up" in orderly fashion. Americans, by contrast, are unruly customers. They will hunt for the fastest line, or look for ways to avoid the line altogether. In a competitive land of opportunity, being special or different is acceptable, even admirable. "Nice guys," we are told, "finish last." Individuals from a society with a greater sense of social unity and solidarity (Norwegians for example) often have exactly the opposite view. They want to be part of the group. They want to share. We like individual choice and control.

These views interact with our attitudes toward new technology. Americans want unlimited access—at their own initiative—to the "best." Consider the case of Magnetic Resonance Imaging (or MRI) machines. Such machines cost $1.5 to $2.5 million to purchase and the current cost per image is now $600 to $700. In some cases, they do offer better pictures than conventional X-rays for soft tissue. All of Canada has about the same number of machines as the city of Boston, and yet Canada has more than ten times as many people—even if we count the entire Boston metropolitan area.

The Siren Call of Technology

The last example brings us face to face with the role of technology in health care. I observe this personally every few weeks. One of the places I teach, the Harvard School of Public Health, is located next to the Harvard Medical School and in the midst of the complex of no less than five teaching hospitals. Whenever I leave after an evening seminar—even at ten o'clock at night—the lights are on in all of the laboratories. What is going on behind those warmly glowing rectangles? *Who* is working there and *what* are they doing?

As to *who,* each of those laboratories is headed by the intellectual equivalent of a member of the U.S. Olympic team; individuals of unusual ability who have achieved their positions as the result of a nationwide competition extending over many years. They did well in high school and went to college (often the most competitive colleges), did well in college and went to medical school (often the most competitive medical schools), and then they got their pick of the best residency training and laboratory research opportunities. Now, finally, having done well yet again, they are faculty members at one of the nation's most prestigious biomedical research institutions.

And *what* are they doing there late on a cold and rainy evening in November? What are they doing, in shiny new facilities chock full of the best equipment on the planet? They are doing scientific research or looking for new ways to cure disease, but what they will ultimately find are new ways to spend health care dollars! Will they be successful? My money is on them. Indeed all of our money is on them, in more ways than one! They and their counterparts, around the country and around the world, have found and will continue to find new ways to spend money. After all, many of today's diagnostic and treatment devices and techniques were unknown forty years ago.

Many of these brilliant young scientists are doing "basic research" that may not have an immediate application. Yet those who defend (and fund) such research always argue that it does "pay off" in the long run—and it is all of us who will do the paying.

Technological change does not *have* to cost more money. Antibiotics or polio vaccines, at least in the short run, decreased costs. So have some drugs that have made expensive surgery less necessary—such as new treatments for stomach ulcers. Also, some labor-saving devices lower labor costs by more than the added cost of the device itself (e.g., bedside computers for better record keeping). Still, a high proportion of medical care inventions serve to increase costs, even as they claim to offer improved performance in return.

The difference can be seen by looking again at the "payoff function" we discussed earlier. As we see in Figure 3, some new technology is "performance and cost increasing." It moves up

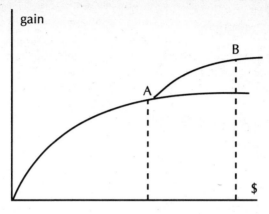

Figure 3

the upper end of the payoff function—allowing us to do what we couldn't do before. As a result we move from point A to point B. Heart transplants are such an innovation. In contrast, cost-reducing technical change shifts the lower part of the cure to the left, as in Figure 4. This allows us to go from C to D to do what we could do before but at lower cost.

Alas, the world offers much greater incentives to biomedical researchers to produce "performance-enhancing" versus "cost-reducing" innovations. The profit potential of the former is much greater. The developer of a unique drug, device, or procedure that can save previously unsavable lives can charge a great deal! If an innovation is simply a less costly alternative to an existing drug or device, the price of the older option limits the price of the new one. Sales volume is likely to depend on offering buyers substantial savings, which significantly limits potential profits.

Moreover, professional prestige and social status depend on *get prestige from inventing* doing what has not been done before. Those who push back the frontiers of science and technology get Nobel Prizes and professorships at famous universities. These rewards are not for those who merely find ways to lower the costs of widely used routine medical procedures.

Government bears great responsibility for this pattern. Almost half the money for biomedical research comes from public funds. Although decisions about how to allocate funds to different

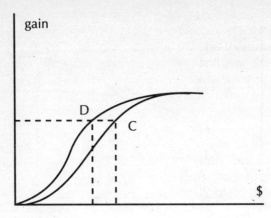

Figure 4

(handwritten margin note, left side: "gov't funds 1/2 of research")

problems are made administratively, within each area grants are generally distributed through an elaborate system of "peer-review." Panels of experts are convened by government agencies to decide, on the merits, what should be funded. Such systems are designed to prevent favoritism and pork barrel politics. But they also have the effect of expressing the values of the scientists in the funding process. And what most technical groups value is "performance-enhancing" change.

The patent system also plays a role. Any drug or device that can benefit from patent protection can enjoy a seventeen-year monopoly. The lure of such monopoly profits provides the incentive for companies to spend tens of millions of dollars on research projects that do not always pay off. Thus our system for financing industrial research depends on companies receiving high, even exorbitant profits on successful innovations: a pattern that has in turn sparked much controversy in recent years. (We return to this issue in Chapter 6.)

New technology can also be quite profitable to practitioners who use it. Surgeons get fees for performing new operations. Radiologists get fees for employing new imaging machines, etc. While new drugs have long required FDA approval, and some medical devices now do also, procedures are largely unregulated. As a result, new surgical techniques can diffuse quite quickly, especially if they are well reimbursed.

(handwritten margin note, left side: "Procedures are largely unregulated")

Consider coronary artery bypass graft surgery. In that procedure, a vein is removed from the leg and grafted onto one or more coronary arteries to improve blood flow to the heart. The procedure was first reported in the literature in 1971. In 1989, the last year for which we have data, over 360,000 were done, at an average cost of $46,000 (for a total of over $16 billion). Meanwhile, there has been great controversy over how sick an individual should be before receiving the surgery. Here was clinical ambiguity with a vengeance. It took a whole series of careful clinical trials over ten years to clarify when the surgery is in fact indicated. At least at one point, some authorities were urging that 15 to 20 percent of the procedures being done were inappropriate because the medical risks outweighed the medical benefits, given that the operative mortality rate averaged 5 percent.

Because the overall cost impact of an innovation is difficult to disentangle, the numbers thrown around in public debate can be quite misleading. First, the largest costs of a new technology—say a new imaging machine like an MRI—are not simply the costs of the machine itself. Instead, the salaries of all those who operate, repair, schedule patients for, and interpret the results of the machine are typically much greater than the annual capital costs of the machine itself. Add in the cost of material, supplies, and space and you can begin to see the complex cost implications.

For example, suppose the MRI costs $2 million. If we depreciate it over ten years ($200,000 a year) and finance it at 8 percent ($160,000 a year), the annual capital costs of the machine itself would be $360,000. This could easily be swamped by the $700,000 to $900,000 in operating costs required to support all the technicians, temple acolytes, and high priests who service the machine.

Of course, the MRI might substitute for other imaging devices and so lead to cost offsets elsewhere. But more frequently, clinical uncertainty and social attitudes (not to mention reimbursement) lead doctors to use both the old technology and the new. Of course, health might be improved by this added spending. But several studies—especially of imaging devices—suggest that new technology does not always provide information that leads to meaningful differences in treatment. (Given our limited medical knowledge and treatment capacity, such a result should not be that surprising.)

Indeed, improved technology can sometimes even lead to less desirable outcomes. Consider the use of fetal heart monitors, attached to the scalp of an about-to-be-born infant. Such devices seemed to offer the prospect of telling doctors when to do Cesarean sections to alleviate infant cardiac distress. We now know that those monitors contributed to an inappropriate and costly rise in "C-sections" and to the unhappiness of many mothers who did not have normal deliveries.

This was the result of a phenomenon called "false positives"—test results that indicate a problem that in fact is not there. Such mistakes are inevitable with any real world, imperfect test. Accepting a certain rate of false positives is the only way to minimize the opposite error of failing to detect a problem that is there (a "false negative"). But the result can be still further, inappropriate interventions or unnecessary tests as the initial results are acted upon. To help counteract such problems, many doctors and hospitals now restrict the use of such monitors to those cases where they are specifically medically indicated.

Another example of the false positive problem became apparent when new devices for doing many blood tests at once—so-called multichannel analyzers—were first developed some decades ago. Physicians (especially doctors in their training residencies) got used to ordering, and looking at, all ten or twenty results that were automatically produced each time they needed one test. The resulting, entirely predictable false positives led to many needless and costly further investigations. As a result, many teaching hospitals no longer even have forms that let residents order the whole battery of tests simply by checking one box. These institutions now also don't report to doctors the results of tests not explicitly ordered, even if the machines in the laboratory have done such tests automatically.

Computing the costs of a new technology is made more complicated by the need to consider its potentially wide-ranging effects on the whole health care system. Many early studies of organ transplantation, for example, looked only at the costs of the hospitalization during which the transplant occurred. Yet there are significant pretransplant screening costs—and these costs (including those patients who are never transplanted) arguably should be averaged into the cost of each transplant ultimately performed. Moreover, the largest costs of a transplant actually occur after the operation itself. These are the costs of drugs, lab work, and rehospitalization during those episodes when the body rejects the transplanted organ. Some have also argued that the cost of a successful transplant should be calculated in a way that includes a share of the costs for those transplants that don't succeed. Conversely, we avoid, and hence should subtract the costs we would have paid for caring for transplanted individuals if they had not been transplanted. And if all this were not confusing enough, the available data are of very limited accuracy because they are based on hospital bills—not on what it actually costs the hospital to provide the services in question.

In sum, biomedical research produces a steady stream of new things on which to spend health care dollars. Moreover, these innovations generally increase costs in the search for better care. By doing so, scientists and entrepreneurs are simply following the Willie Sutton principle. When asked why he robbed banks, Willie replied, "Because that's where the money is." If health care reform is to alter the kinds of technological change the system produces, we are going to have to offer those involved different incentives. Otherwise they will simply continue to function happily in their existing ecological niches within the health care swamp.

The Politics of Health Care

In a famous speech in 1960, the late Dwight Eisenhower, hardly a social radical, warned the nation about the influence of the "military industrial complex." In health care, there is a "medical industrial complex" that can be particularly troublesome when the goal is cost containment. It is important to remember that every health care cost is someone else's health care income. And those income recipients can be counted on to battle mightily to preserve their advantages.

The point was well made by the late Lyndon Johnson. The occasion was a discussion of efforts designed to close the tax "loopholes" that made oil drilling more profitable in his home state of Texas (the infamous "oil depletion allowance"). "One man's loophole," said Johnson, "is another man's living."

The health care industry is now approximately 14 percent of the Gross Domestic Product—the largest industry in the country. There are 1.6 million nurses and 600,000 doctors. There are more than 5,500 hospitals and 1,200 insurance companies. Then there are the drug companies and the medical device manufacturers, not to mention the architects, building contractors, food suppliers, and data processing companies that all depend on health care. Many of these organizations have substantial experience in lobbying—and have organized Political Action Committees (or PACs) that make substantial contributions to senators and congressmen.

Moreover, every congressional district has one or more hospitals and every member of Congress has prominent physicians in his or her district who are both local opinion leaders and potential campaign contributors. Indeed, hospitals and doctors command all the resources necessary for effective political action: money, votes, the ability to call on committed campaign workers, loyalists with media access and communications skills, individuals with influence in the community, and so on. Often local business leaders and socially prominent citizens serve on the board of the local hospital, and they along with doctors, nurses, blue-collar workers, and community volunteers can all be mobilized on its behalf. And then there are former patients and/or families—who want to protect "Hometown-General-Hospital-where-they-were-so-nice-to-us-when-Aunt-Ginny-was-so-sick-that-time."

In the last presidential election, all the Democratic primary candidates were quick to pledge support for building another Seawolf submarine in order to protect 8,000 jobs in Groton, Connecticut. Now, the Seawolf is designed to hunt down those Soviet subs that are trying to hunt down our ballistic missile subs that are there to discourage the Russians from launching a nuclear first strike. How much sense does all that make with the Russian missiles being dismantled and the Soviet fleet rusting at its moorings in Murmansk and Sevastopol? Yet if the prospect of losing 8,000 jobs in Groton, Connecticut, can do that to a political campaign, what will the prospect of losing 28,000 jobs from the health insurance industry in nearby Hartford, Connecticut, do to mobilize political support against any reform plan that threatened those jobs?

In American interest group politics, those most affected by a policy have the biggest incentive to be involved. Even a small group can have more impact than a much larger group of opponents—especially if each of the latter has only a modest stake in the result. Those who are already organized for other purposes also have an advantage. A trade association, professional ties, mailing lists, telephones, and office staff, all these can make it much easier for the few to out-organize and out-lobby the many.

This pattern helps explain much of the particularism exhibited by American politics. The contractors who will build the manned space station are very well organized and will fight to the death to keep the project alive. The mass of skeptical citizens, each of whom might save sixty dollars if the station were canceled, hardly have the incentive to make a comparable effort to get it terminated.

Exactly the same situation obtains in health care. Those who gain from the current system are very well organized and have a very large stake in the outcome of any reform effort. Those who merely pay the bill are much less well organized. Business and government, as we saw in Chapter 1, do have a significant stake in reform. But for any company—or government—health care reform is only one of many pressing issues. For those in the health business, however, health care reform is far and away the most important issue—even the only issue. Furthermore, government and business groups, exactly because they have so many concerns, often cannot match the providers in depth and breadth of expertise.

We have also seen how corporate participation is made more difficult by the fact that different companies may have very different interests. Small businesses paying high insurance rates will favor "community rating" so that they can be cross-subsidized. Large businesses, which now benefit from "experience rating" or that self-insure, will have every reason to oppose such a scheme.

In our political system, a new and alternative future is not likely to be at the table when political bargaining takes place.

That is why the shape of health care reform is still uncertain. Will the cost pressures on government and business be enough to induce them to mobilize to counteract provider interests? Or will the providers be able to defend themselves, especially when the relevant congressional committee staffs meet to hammer out the details? This matters greatly, as we will see in Chapters 5 and 6. Health care reform is one arena where the statement of the great architect Ludwig Mies van der Rohe certainly holds true. Speaking of design, he said, "The devil is in the details."

Finally, contemporary American political attitudes will also surely shape health care reform. These include a skepticism about government action, a strong antipathy toward new taxes, and widespread suspicion of any statement made by a public official. Humor reveals a lot about how the public is thinking. And most readers probably know the joke that begins with "What are the three biggest lies in the world," and ends with "I'm from the government and I'm here to help you."

Such fiscal and functional conservatism has not always dominated American politics. The Roosevelt coalition gave an activist Democratic Party control over national politics for the best part of more than thirty years—through the end of the Johnson administration. But after the transitional Nixon-Ford-Carter period, Ronald Reagan took advantage of underlying forces to provoke and reinforce a major change in the political landscape. He convinced much of the blue-collar, Northern industrial, traditionally Democratic vote to support him. He did so based on two arguments. One was anticommunism. The other was the claim that the beneficiaries of social programs were undeserving and that unionized blue-collar workers would lose more than they would gain from such programs. At the same time, many of the sons and daughters of these staunchly Democratic urban immigrants had already moved to the suburbs and up the economic ladder—becoming more conservative in the process.

Other things have also changed in American politics. The South is increasingly prepared to forgive the Republicans for being the party of Lincoln and Reconstruction—and to vote its regional conservative ideology in place of its historic loyalty. The small farmers of the Midwest are disappearing, being replaced by large "agri-business" that looks increasingly Republican. Indeed agriculture has become our most capital-intensive industry with more capital per worker (in land, building, and equipment) than even oil refining. Thus, as Clinton represents, the political center of gravity now seems more clearly in the center. And health care reform will have to respond to that shift.

The success of Ronald Reagan's political revisionism has left other marks on the current debate. If government is the problem, how can government act effectively to clean up the health care crisis? If taxation is illegitimate, how can we raise taxes to pay for the care of those who cannot pay for themselves? Interestingly enough, polling data reveal that Americans are more likely to trust government to undertake health care reform than any of the other institutional alternatives. Yet these same pools suggest Americans are willing to spend only twenty-five or fifty dollars per year in higher taxes to contribute to such a solution.

Moreover, the years of being told that all government fiscal problems were due to fraud and mismanagement have begun to influence attitudes toward health care as well. Most Americans seem to believe that only modest added costs would be required if only waste, inefficiency, profiteering, and inappropriately high compensation were eliminated from the health care system. So any potential coalition of nonproviders will enter into the political fray having to respond to these (quite mistaken) popular views. As we have said repeatedly, health care reform will not be easy.

The Current Dilemma

Where does this review of the underlying causes of the health care crisis leave us? We began with clinical ambiguity. In some fraction of cases doctors don't know exactly what to do, in large part because that is quite difficult to find out. No wonder patterns of practice vary! That ambiguity is reinforced by, and intersects with the changing pattern of disease. As we have gone from infectious disease to chronic developmental and degenerative conditions, we face ever more difficult choices over how much to do for any given patient.

In solving these policy problems, we have to recognize the role played in our thinking and our practice by America's faith in technology in general and in medical technology in particular. In

...ed with youth we increasingly rely on ever more
...dical techno-magic to save us (and our loved ones)
...ty and from the inevitable reality of death. Think how
...e honest and upsetting it would be if we never talked
abo... gains from health programs in terms of "lives saved,"
and instead characterized such benefits as "deaths postponed"!

Still, as a society we want the latest and the best, and we want it on our own terms. New devices may continue to raise costs to unaffordable heights, but we heap praise on the discoverers and fill our media with stories whose theme is "Gosh, another medical miracle." Is it any wonder that so many AIDS activists are so distressed at the failure of biomedical science to solve their terrifying problem? From where, but our own health care system, have they gotten their expectations?

Furthermore, any change in this system will encounter fierce resistance from those with the largest stake in the status quo. On the other side is a set of overburdened would-be reformers who have much else to worry about, and who are operating in a political culture that ranges from the ambivalent to the hostile when it comes to new public programs and the taxes to fund them. All of this makes engineering a successful response to the current crisis a daunting prospect.

Our next task is to examine how the health care system itself is organized and operates. What are the major structural features of that system, and how do those features influence its behavior? So far, we have been circling over the swamp in an airplane, looking at its broad features. Now it's time to set out by airboat, canoe, and on foot if necessary, to get a closer look.

3

THE STRUCTURE OF THE U.S. HEALTH CARE SYSTEM:
How It Works (and Doesn't Work)

Someone Is Paying the Piper

When Bob Woodward and Carl Bernstein were investigating the Watergate burglary, their inside source, code-named "Deep Throat," told them "Follow the money." That is how this chapter proceeds. It begins with the evolution of the private health insurance industry and then explores the functioning of Medicare and Medicaid. Then we focus on how doctors and hospitals are actually paid for care and the incentives that system creates for all producers in the system.

Imagine what it would be like to walk into an exclusive New York restaurant secure in the knowledge that you had "restaurant insurance." The owner would usher you to a table, all the while telling you that you certainly deserved "the best." He will order for you, he suggests, because he is an expert, the one who really knows the menu. You will start with the caviar—expensive now with all the trouble in Russia and Iran—but after all, you *are* insured! After outlining a wonderful set of dishes he concludes by suggesting out-of-season strawberries flown in from Chile and an excellent vintage dry Taittinger champagne for dessert. The champagne, he shrugs, is admittedly also very expensive. But the specialist he has called in for consultation (the wine waiter) assures him that it is the perfect complement to the strawberries. "Under the circumstances," he says, "the sommelier's professional judgment is that champagne is clearly indicated."

As he bustles off to the kitchen to arrange for all of this, he offers you his congratulations on having had the foresight to sign up for such a generous "Blue Plate" insurance plan. He does not mention what the bill will be, and in fact you may never even see it. Nor does he call attention to the fact that he takes a 300 percent markup on the champagne—to help cover the costs of his less profitable activities—nor that the wine waiter "specialist" is getting a percentage of gross wine sales. If all this sounds fanciful, just wait!

Paying for health care in the United States relies on a very complex, Rube Goldberg–like set of arrangements. Close to 75 percent of the nonelderly have at least some private health insurance, while nearly 10 percent are covered by Medicaid and about 18 percent are uninsured. Almost all citizens over sixty-five are covered by Medicare. However, almost 70 percent of that population also have some private insurance, and 9 percent are also covered by Medicaid. (Medicare and Medicaid are discussed in more detail in the next section.)

These percentages, however, give a misleading impression of the financial role of private insurance. Fully 40 percent of all personal health care expenditures come from government sources, and only about one third are paid for by private insurance. Patients pay about one fourth of the total out-of-pocket. In another sense, of course, individuals pay the entire bill. They pay for public and private insurance through taxes or their own insurance premium payments. They also pay for employer contributions to private insurance through lower wages or through the higher prices they pay as customers for a company's products.

The private insurance sector is both very complicated and in the midst of a rapid transition. The traditionally most powerful organizations, the Blue Cross plans that had 60 to 70 percent market shares in many Northern and Eastern states, are struggling

*[handwritten margin note: 40% expenses paid by gov't
1/4 by out of pocket
1/4 by private insurance.
30% by private insurance]*

to maintain their viability. A whole host of new "insurance products" is being offered by a bewildering variety of competitors, including the commercial insurance companies, various "health maintenance organizations" (a term we explain shortly), and new sellers, like hospital consortiums. The options—and the jargon—seem overwhelming, even for the well informed.

How America Got "the Blues"

The first important steps toward creating the current mess occurred during the Great Depression. Hospitals, like everyone else, found that customers often could not pay their bills, especially once they got sick. Existing health insurance schemes were small and scattered. Commercial companies had found the market unprofitable and there were only a few other plans sponsored by fraternal and community organizations. In 1929, Dr. Justin Kimball at Baylor University Hospital in Dallas, Texas, devised what seemed like a terrific answer. Why not get people to pay for their care *before* they got sick, while they could afford the payments—in effect, a contractual savings plan sort of like the Christmas Clubs at banks. He began with a group of 1,250 schoolteachers.

The American Hospital Association, and its various affiliated state associations, rapidly expanded upon Kimball's idea. Between 1930 and 1933, they developed a whole series of principles governing such plans and soon thereafter began lobbying state legislatures to adopt enabling statutes that gave the new organizations—called "Blue Cross" plans—special legal status.

Several features of these organizations distinguished them from commercial insurance companies—apart from their own fierce insistence that they were different. (That insistence led them to adopt their own terminology, different from that used by other insurance companies.) The "Blues" were nonprofit entities with interlocking boards of directors that connected them with their state hospital associations.

Blue Cross plans were initially dedicated to the idea that all "subscribers" (not "customers") would pay the same fee—so-called "community rating"—regardless of their health status. This was one way to deal with the noninsurability of health risks.

Simply ignore which houses were on fire. Such an approach—in which the healthy cross-subsidized the sick because they all paid the same premiums—suited the hospitals since it allowed them to collect enough to cover their costs.

Blue Cross coverage spread very rapidly in the 1930s and 1940s, in part in response to a series of other economic policies. First, the National Industrial Recovery Act, and then the National Labor Relations Act, created formal government mechanisms for recognizing the role of unions in collective bargaining. Health care was a major concern of those unions and they pushed for health insurance benefits. Many unions became strong supporters of Blue Cross, and even had representatives on various local plans' boards of directors.

In addition, the system of wage and price controls imposed during World War II exempted fringe benefits. This gave both labor and management a great incentive to provide compensation by means of health insurance. As income tax rates rose, the IRS decided in 1954 that employers' health insurance contributions should not be counted as part of an employee's taxable income. This too gave companies an incentive to provide increased compensation in the form of health insurance, since it enabled them to do so tax free. Despite its initial reluctance, the AMA ultimately authorized the development of similar plans for physician services—called Blue Shield plans. (Now most such plans are sold as a package with Blue Cross by integrated organizations.)

In response to growing demand, the commercial insurance companies came back into the market. To limit their own risks, they often provided incentives to their customers to limit claims. Thus they frequently sold coverage that included "deductibles"— the customer paid the first X dollars—or "co-insurance"—the customer paid X percent up to some limit. They also often had an upper limit to the total amount they would pay. And, in the early days, they typically reimbursed their policyholders after the fact.

Blue Cross, in contrast, true to its hospital origins, paid hospitals directly. And initially most plans emphasized "first-dollar" coverage—without significant deductibles, co-pays, or limits. From the hospital's point of view, such policies made sense. They allowed the hospital to avoid the expensive and perhaps unsuccessful effort of collecting bills from the patient. Because of their special legal status in many states, the Blues often paid less for care than did their competitors; the hospitals frequently gave them a special discount, permitting them to pay less than costs. Other insurers paid full costs or charges, which were well above costs.

The commercial companies, however, continued to gain market share, in part because they offered to set premiums on the basis of each large employer's actual experience. Since the workers in these companies tended to be healthier than the population as a whole, "experience-rated" premiums were generally below the Blue Cross "community rate." If the group were large enough, the uninsurability problem could be handled by ignoring variations in individual risk within the group, and selling insurance to the whole group at a single rate. In the course of the postwar period, the Blues were often forced to copy these underwriting practices.

Over time, the cozy relationship between Blue Cross and the American Hospital Association (and Blue Shield and the AMA) resulted in increasing criticism. But a complete divorce didn't take place between the two until the 1970s. The boards of directors of the organizations were disentangled and the Blue Cross Association obtained control over the Blue Cross trademark—which the AHA had previously owned and controlled.

Today, the relative role of Blue Cross and the commercial insurance companies varies by region and industrial sector. Manufacturing companies in heavily unionized industries, and government workers, particularly in the Northeast and the upper Midwest, are more likely to have Blue Cross coverage. In many regions, however, Blue Cross plans have been in real trouble recently. Some observers attribute their decline to poor internal management, to a lack of organizational discipline and competitive instinct made possible by years of special privileges and favorable treatment. The cost of their traditional plans has increased significantly as health care costs have risen. And they have been slow to match the new insurance products introduced by commercial companies. Managerial scandals, and the fact that state law often requires the Blues to accept everyone in return for their organizational privileges, have also played a role in their decline.

Henry Kaiser to the Rescue

Meanwhile, another set of insurance providers was emerging—a group whose appearance has decisively influenced the current policy debate. Ironically, the "new" and "radical" idea that these were based on was the transformation of an "old" and "reactionary" system—the company-organized health care system!

A key pioneer here was Henry Kaiser, one of the last great American industrialists. In the 1930s, as he was expanding in both the steel and cement industries in California, he started an innovative company health care system for his growing work force. He contracted with groups of full-time physicians to provide all the care that his employees required, even building his own clinics and hospitals for them to practice in. Physicians worked on salary with bonuses to provide productivity incentives. As a result, the entire system could be staffed, planned for, and budgeted like any other business activity.

Kaiser's activities, including shipbuilding, expanded greatly during World War II and so did his health care organization. After the war, the Kaiser-Permanente Health Care System was "spun off" as an independent nonprofit corporation. It also began to provide health care for other companies. The Kaiser work force had begun to shrink from its wartime high and the Kaiser health care system had excess capacity. By then, it had expanded up and down the West Coast and into Hawaii.

There were other organizations, in other parts of the country, that to varying degrees resembled Kaiser. HIP in New York provided physician but not hospital services. The Mayo Clinic, in Rochester, Minnesota, was a multispecialty group of salaried doctors. But it did not offer total coverage for a fixed fee. The San Joaquin Foundation in Southern California became the model for what were called "Independent Practice Associations," or IPAs. These were associations of independently practicing physicians who offered benefits and services comparable to Kaiser, but in their own offices.

In 1973, as part of a health care cost-containment effort, President Nixon, with congressional cooperation, legislatively expanded the role of these various organizations. They were now labeled "Health Maintenance Organizations" or HMOs. The theory was that HMOs would be more efficient than the so-called "fee-for-service" sector. Since they received "capitated" payment—that is, so much per person per year—they had every incentive to provide care more cheaply. In some sense, they would be closer to a cost-conscious college dining hall—operating on a fixed budget—than the fee-for-service restaurant we conjured up initially.

HMOs could control costs in various ways. In a "staff model" scheme like Kaiser, doctors are on salary, removing any incentive to do more. In many IPAs, if volume is above planned levels, the amount doctors are paid for each unit of service is adjusted proportionately downward. Also, the primary care doctor within the HMO system could act as a "gatekeeper"—controlling utilization of more expensive specialist services. The HMO could also run its own efficient hospitals, or negotiate low prices from independent hospitals—since the latter wanted the HMOs' large-volume business. And on the outpatient side, effective management and quality control systems were supposed to allow them to operate more efficiently.

The other theory was that HMOs would spend money on screening and prevention. This would enable them to act immediately to "maintain the health" of their members and thereby avoid the future high costs of caring for untreated disease. This too was supposed to lower overall costs.

To qualify for federal help under the 1973 legislation, an HMO had to offer comprehensive benefits and meet other criteria. Yet despite this aid, over the next twenty years, the HMOs' market share grew only slowly, to about 15 percent in most areas. Central to this slow growth has been customer dissatisfaction with HMOs' cost-control efforts. Free choice of doctor (and hospital) is often limited—especially in "staff model" plans. Referrals to specialists are often tightly controlled and available only after some delays. And salaried staff can be less concerned with keeping patients happy than doctors whose incomes depend directly on their reputation for service.

A psychiatrist friend told me about a lawyer he took under treatment when the latter became dissatisfied with his HMO. The lawyer's problem was serious—unresolved self-destructive tendencies were leading him to embezzle large sums from his own firm's operating funds. His HMO assigned him to group therapy, which does cost a lot less than individual psychotherapy. But the lawyer was not about to tell a group of eight strangers about the thievery he was committing. He wasn't *that* crazy!

I personally have found myself on a pay phone in the lobby of my own HMO, calling a plan executive I know to try to get better service. For example, one of my sons once suffered from a mysterious and possibly serious soccer injury that his pediatrician found puzzling. I was told there was nearly a three-week wait to see the orthopedist whom the pediatrician had referred him to. When I complained of the delay, my friend explained that orthopedists were expensive and that the plan couldn't find enough willing to work at the salaries it was willing to pay. He then arranged for an out-of-plan referral. But suppose I hadn't known someone "higher up"?

There has also been quite a bit of reconsideration of the "health maintenance" feature of HMOs. Widespread screening tends to increase an HMO's short-run costs since conditions are discovered that then require treatment. The potential gains from any future cost savings, in contrast, tend to be both long delayed and quite uncertain. After all, current members might well switch to other insurance plans in the interim.

Managing the Sick

Nonetheless, in recent years, HMOs in various forms have increased their market share. As costs have increased, the financial advantages of such plans have become increasingly attractive. In addition, fewer and fewer companies even offer employees insurance plans with totally unlimited choice of providers. For example, an employer will offer an insurance plan that will pay full costs if the employee uses a provider in a specified "network," but a lesser share if the employee goes elsewhere. And providers in the "network" are chosen for their capacity and willingness to control utilization. It is like the restaurant insurers limiting their customers to the less extravagant establishments.

New insurance plan sponsors have also proliferated. Many of the Blues have begun to offer various "managed-care products." Also, many individual or groups of hospitals now sponsor their own HMOs. A growing number of large employers have even become their own insurers.

This last development is in part because of a federal statute called ERISA (Employee Retirement Income and Security Act of 1974), which limits state regulation of certain company- and union-sponsored pension plans and benefit funds. This law has allowed company-organized plans to escape much state insurance regulation—and more than half of all group insurance coverage is now provided in this way. One obvious advantage to companies which provide their own plans is that they know they will not be paying for the medical costs of someone else's employees. If a company has a relatively large and healthy work force, it can spread its limited risk over its own work force and "self-insure." (This is like a restaurant insurance pool that caters mainly to small, skinny people.) In the process the company can design its own plan, which the insurance company merely administers.

This development helps explain why many companies now offer plans that will not pay for the costs of "preexisting conditions" for a given time period. As self-insurers, the costs of caring for such illnesses come directly out of a company's profits. Moreover, such exclusions discourage sick workers from seeking employment with the company in question, further lowering its long-run costs.

All of these corporate cost-control efforts have placed increased burdens on individuals, which, as we have seen, has helped provoke the current political interest in health care reform. Workers now pay more for their insurance, and to add "injury to injury," they now often have to pay more in co-insurance and deductibles each time they seek care.

Insurance companies have also greatly strengthened their efforts at "risk management"—which in practice means encouraging sick people to join someone else's plan. The story is told, perhaps apocryphally, of a California HMO that had its enrollment offices on the third floor of a building without elevators. They would take anyone who could walk up the two flights! Another story concerns an HMO whose specialists in certain high-cost areas were technically impeccably qualified—but were foreign-trained physicians with imperfect English language skills. The not-so-subtle goal was to encourage high-cost patients to enroll in other plans.

Yet another insurance company response has been to require doctors or hospitals to get prior approval before undertaking certain treatments, or before keeping a patient in the hospital an extra day. It is like asking the restaurant owner to get approval from the ultimate bill payer for the menu he has devised—a step that would be quite likely to limit the consumption of caviar and champagne!

The result of all these efforts has been to raise the health care system's *administrative* costs. The various new review processes employ many, many people in both the insurance companies and on the part of providers. And many of these individuals are paid to argue with each other. Military planners refer to an army's "tooth to tail" ratio—the fraction of the force that fights (tooth) versus supports (tail). If we apply the same idea to health care, caring (tooth) versus support (tail) in the United States comes out quite badly.

The self-employed and those in small business, where many of America's new jobs are created, have confronted special problems. This is the result of "adverse selection," a phenomenon that again reflects the noninsurability of health care costs. In a large corporation, enough individuals are insured for the health care costs of the group to be relatively stable—even in the face of serious illness experienced by a few members.

In contrast some small groups have higher than average health care costs because they include a few unfortunate members. Those groups are exactly the ones most likely to purchase insurance. Insurance companies have traditionally treated the small group and individual policyholders as a single risk pool for underwriting purposes. Since those who purchased insurance tended to be sicker than average, their premiums have tended to be quite high. Discouraged by such rates, those who knew they were healthy have often dropped their insurance. The sick felt they had no choice and stayed in the pool—whose loss experience only worsened, setting off additional rate increases and still more withdrawals.

In the insurance business the result is called the "adverse selection death spiral." In response some insurance companies have begun to set separate rates for small groups with poor loss experience, or even deny them coverage altogether.

The resulting confusion and high rates have made "small market reform" central to many state health care reform efforts. But policies designed simply to lower administrative costs (by, say, forming purchasing cooperatives) will not sufficiently lower rates unless a way is found to deal with the adverse selection problem. Somehow, various groups of healthier people will have to be merged into this pool—either from within, or outside small business—if the average loss, and premium, is to come down.

In some regions of the country, the small business problem has been made even more difficult by the development of AIDS. As the disease has spread in the gay community, it has hit parts of the small business sector especially hard. As a result of these costs, as well as a tendency toward high rates of industrial accidents in other sectors, the small business loss experience has been especially high in certain specific lines of business. Insurance companies have responded with techniques like "sectoral redlining"—not covering any firm in some industry—in order to limit their losses. Moreover, businesses with many low-paid seasonal or short-term workers (like agriculture or construction) find it both difficult and uneconomic to purchase insurance.

It is also worth noting that many of those who work in small businesses are in what is sometimes called "the secondary labor market." These are individuals who because of the kind of work they do (like small construction), labor market discrimination, or their own preferences, tend to move frequently from one job to another, and into and out of employment. Trying to cover these individuals under any employment-based insurance system will obviously not be easy administratively.

Pumping Nutrients into the Swamp—Medicare and Medicaid

The 40 percent of personal health care expenditures that government pays flows primarily through two main programs—

Medicare and Medicaid. Medicare and Medicaid were added to the Social Security Act in 1965, under titles 18 and 19, after an epic political battle. They extended public financing to those groups that arguably had the greatest difficulty financing their own care—even through the "Christmas Club" arrangements of Blue Cross—namely the elderly and the poor.

In the course of the battle over Medicare and Medicaid, providers ultimately became reconciled to expanded public financing. Public payment—however much it smacked of "socialized medicine"—seemed better than no payment at all. Indeed, providers were ultimately able to extract quite generous language in the initial legislation describing how they were to be paid. This no doubt made the whole idea easier to accept.

The two programs are quite different. Medicare has two parts. Part A provides coverage for hospital costs for essentially all of those over sixty-five. Part B, which is optional, covers physician costs for those who choose to pay the premiums. Hospital benefits are financed out of the same federal payroll tax that supports the Social Security Trust Funds. The tax rate for Medicare is currently 1.45 percent on both employers and employees or 2.9% of wages overall. What many people don't realize is that general tax revenues support the cost of Part B coverage, which is chosen by more than 90 percent of those who are eligible. Medicare also covers various special categories of disabled patients under sixty-five, including a targeted program for those with kidney disease (called the End Stage Renal Disease or ESRD program).

Medicare is not a fully comprehensive program. Many services, like nursing home care, eye care, and outpatient drugs, are not covered. There are also various co-insurance and deductible requirements that on average amount to 17 percent of the cost of the services that are covered. Add in what is not covered at all, and Medicare covers less than half the medical care costs of the elderly. As a result, about 68 percent of Medicare recipients have "gap-filling" private insurance, purchased either by themselves or by their former employers. In part, this is to guard themselves against potentially high uncovered costs.

Medicaid, in contrast, is a joint federal-state program. The federal share varies from 50 to 80 percent, depending on a state's income, with higher rates for poorer states. States construct their own Medicaid programs, within broad limits set by federal policy. State participation in Medicaid is optional, and in fact, Arizona did not join the program until 1982.

The largest group of Medicaid recipients are mothers and children, many of whom are also eligible for Aid to Families with Dependent Children. All these participants comprise about 70 percent of all recipients. (In fact the link of Medicaid eligibility to AFDC eligibility creates great problems for welfare reform, since the prospect of losing Medicaid coverage is a major disincentive to increased work among welfare recipients.) There are two other covered groups, the blind and disabled who are eligible for SSI (Supplemental Security Income) benefits and certain poor individuals over sixty-five.

One especially interesting feature of Medicare is its relatively low administrative costs. These now run at 4 percent of total costs or even less, well below the 5.5 percent reported by even the largest private insurers and the 14 percent that is the average in the private insurance sector. In part this is because there are no selling or underwriting expenses. These low costs are achieved by a system of "contracting out." Private sector entities act as the "intermediaries" in each region. It is Federal Express, not the post office, and all things considered, it seems to run reassurably well.

Medicare is the larger program both in dollars and in recipients. In 1991 there were about 35 million Medicare recipients, of whom nearly 5 million were under sixty-five, compared to 25 million enrolled in Medicaid. Medicare spent $120 billion while vendor payments by Medicaid were $100 billion.

The two programs spend money quite differently. Even though Medicare is for the elderly, Medicaid spends a lot more on nursing homes. Only 25 percent of all Medicaid spending goes to hospitals (including outpatient care), doctors get about 6 percent, and nearly 40 percent is spent on various kinds of nursing homes and "intermediate care facilities" (with a large share of that for care for the retarded). In fact, Medicaid provides nearly half of all nursing home revenue. This explains why the 30 percent of Medicaid recipients who are blind, disabled, or aged consume 70 percent of the funds, while the 70 percent of

Medicaid recipients who are poor women and their children account for less than 30 percent of Medicaid spending.

For Medicare, in contrast, over 60 percent of expenditures go for hospital care. Physicians get about 25 percent and nursing homes receive only about 2½ percent. The rest goes to other providers, like laboratories and home health agencies. Thus Medicare pays much more to hospitals and doctors than does Medicaid. So while Medicaid expenditures are of great concern to state governments, and Medicaid payment policies can and do affect the access of the poor to care, Medicare reimbursement rules have a noticeably greater influence on hospital behavior. This is particularly true since other insurers often follow Medicare's lead when it comes to reimbursement policies.

Because Medicaid has been such a major financial problem for the states, they have made many efforts over the years to limit costs. Congress has also tried to hold down federal costs, even while expanding the program to include more women and children. In response, the states have tried to control the increase in their expenditures by cutting benefits, squeezing provider reimbursement, and limiting eligibility to only those groups mandated by the federal government. Both levels of government seek to shift costs to others (especially to the privately insured). This has led some cynical public finance experts to argue that the reality of "fiscal federalism" is actually "shift and shaft."

An interesting example of state cost-control efforts is the effort made by California beginning in the early 1980s to limit hospital choices available to "MediCal" clients (as its Medicaid program was called). The state began to selectively contract with only certain hospitals in each area. The goal was to use its buying leverage to lower program costs. Other states (such as Maryland, New York, and Massachusetts) installed various rate-regulation systems designed in part to limit their Medicaid expenses.

Many of these cost-control efforts (like comparable federal efforts for Medicare) have meant that the programs pay hospitals less than what the hospitals claim are the costs of caring for these patients. The resulting difference is often referred to by hospital administrators as the Medicare/Medicaid "shortfall." Exactly what we should make of that "shortfall" is a complicated matter, however, which we discuss later in the chapter after we have had a chance to describe a bit more about hospital accounting.

The states have had more control over physician payments under Medicaid than the federal government has had under Medicare. To control their costs, therefore, many states have simply lowered the amount they pay physicians for various services. Both legally and politically, this has often been easier than lowering hospital reimbursement. Medicaid recipients are often both medically high risk and can confront providers with the need to make an extra effort to overcome cultural and class differences. In response, many physicians—either formally or informally—have withdrawn from the Medicaid program. Unlike hospitals, which are legally obligated to accept all acutely ill patients, doctors do not have to accept all patients into their practices.

The result has been a lack of access to primary care for many Medicaid recipients. Obstetrics has been especially hard hit. Medicaid clients have therefore tended to make disproportionate use of hospital emergency rooms—where they cannot be turned away—as their basic source of outpatient care. In response a number of states have recently instituted "managed-care" programs for Medicaid recipients, with the goal of linking them to regular sources of care outside of hospital emergency rooms.

Emergency room use does have at least two deleterious effects. The health of individuals can deteriorate because of the lack of follow-up care in such settings. Moreover, emergency rooms are relatively expensive, compared to, say, a physician's office. (The actual cost comparison is more complex than usually acknowledged, and ER costs are typically overstated, for reasons we discuss in the section on hospitals below.)

In sum, the existing public health insurance programs, which cover perhaps 20 percent of the population, only very imperfectly fill in the gaps left by private insurance. As a result 15 percent of the population is uninsured. Many of these individuals are poor; by some estimates 60 percent of the nonaged population under the federal poverty level are not eligible for Medicaid, including most childless, nondisabled adults.

When the uninsured don't pay their hospital bills they are counted as "bad debt and free care" by the institution. Bills of those who could pay but don't are classified as bad debt. Bills of those who can't pay are classified as free care. Until quite recently many hospitals made little effort to distinguish between the two because they wanted to avoid the expense of trying to collect bills, even from those who might reasonably be expected to pay. Instead, they were relatively willing to write off unpaid bills as uncollectible. If hospitals were to break even, some payer had to make up the difference. But increasingly all payers, including Medicare and Medicaid, have refused to do that.

As a result, some states have developed special payment mechanisms to help defray these costs. Generally, funding comes from a surcharge or tax on hospital bills of between 10 percent and 20 percent. Ironically, this mechanism amounts to a "sickness tax." It raises the bills, and hence the insurance premiums, of those who use the hospital most often. More recently, states have recognized that reimbursing hospitals for bad debt only weakens their incentives to collect from patients. So now "free care" funds are often restricted to paying for those patients who, on examination, qualify on economic grounds.

This entire system of public financing, despite its inconsistencies and irrational features, will not be easy to change. Medicaid recipients may not be especially powerful or well organized. The opposite is true, however, for the elderly covered by Medicare. They can be expected to fight to keep their program free of the "entangling alliances" of any national plan, since they believe that they will only lose by such an amalgamation.

Reimbursement: Rewarding the Swamp's Most Effective Predators

Economists are trained to pay attention to the effect of financial incentives on behavior. That effect can be overstated, of course. People do things for many resons. Power, love, status, grand ideals, training, religion, fame, and loyalty all surely matter. But money matters as well. And here the most important fact about the way we pay providers of health care in the United States is also the simplest. Like old-fashioned sweatshop employees, most doctors and hospitals operate on a piecework basis. The more they do, the more they get paid. This fact all too frequently presents providers with a potential conflict of interest. If the right treatment is not clear, and I get paid more for doing more, how can I prevent that from influencing my judgment? (Remember the wine waiter.)

Add into this mix some of the other factors we have already mentioned: American anxieties about death, the steady flow of new things to do (in the form of new technology), and the fact that frightened (and insured) patients typically *want* doctors and hospitals to do more. Together these factors comprise much of the driving force behind the growth of health care to 14 percent of Gross Domestic Product.

I became fully aware of this linkage about ten years ago as a result of the following interesting experience. The full story is a bit circuitous but bear with me. It began one unseasonably warm December afternoon, with the accumulated snow and ice melting in the sunshine. I had just left a shop on Boston's fashionable Newbury Street. Now, I normally carry a cane to compensate for the early effects of polio. But I wasn't using one that day and foolishly tried to step across the water accumulating in the gutter at the corner. I slipped and fell on the melting ice. The fact that I had brought this on myself did not improve my temper when half a second later, I lay in icy water in the gutter. For I had both heard and felt the bone in the hip of my weak leg snap on the way down! A kindly stranger offered to call me a taxi. I asked for an ambulance instead.

The ambulance took me to a hospital near my office. I got the obstetrics resident on duty in the emergency room to call a physician friend on the hospital staff, and that friend recommended a good orthopedic surgeon—who decided not to operate to pin my hip, but just to leave it in traction. The X-rays showed that the broken bone was still well lined up ("nondisplaced," as they say).

I later discovered that this orthopedist had once worked on salary for a local HMO, making much less than he could in the private practice he was then developing. When I saw him some time after my discharge, I asked about that. He said he liked the HMO setting, in part because of cases like mine. He had enjoyed being on salary and hence being free of the conflicts of interest that fee-for-service medicine produced.

If he had operated and pinned my hip, he would have made $2,000. For the consult that led to the traction, he got perhaps $200. There were considerations both ways. In a weak leg, the bone might need the pin to heal. On the other hand, the operative wound might be slow to heal. It was a "gut judgment," he said, about which way to go, and he didn't trust his own gut that much. Suppose he was not very busy someday, and had a college tuition payment coming up? Could he really be sure that only his clinical, and not his financial, instincts were influencing his intuition?

The point of this story is *not* that physicians are inappropriate or unethical income maximizers. Quite the contrary. The point is that we put even the most self-critical and conscientious of them, like this quite wonderful surgeon, in difficult positions because of the way we pay for their services.

This story also illustrates other features of the reimbursement system, notably that we pay doctors more for *doing* than for *thinking*. This creates incentives for specialists to perform well-reimbursed procedures, like gastrointestinal explorations or cardiac catheterization to investigate heart defects. There are also ramifications for the overall rewards offered to different kinds of medical specialties. Historically, certain specialists have been able to earn from three to five times as much as physicians who worked in areas that were not procedure intensive, like pediatrics or psychiatry. And that in turn (as we discuss below) has influenced the whole pattern of medical training.

Medicare payment to physicians was particularly Byzantine. It relied on a combination to the average charge for a particular service in a particular region, and the physician's own billing practices. This produced irrational variations across regions and even among physicians within a region. In response to these difficulties, a new physician payment scheme was adopted by Medicare in 1989. The so-called "resource based relative value scale" (or RBRVS) creates more than 2,000 procedure codes. The relative values attached to each of these are supposed to reflect the time, training, and skill involved. In general, they are intended to provide increased rewards for cognitive as opposed to procedure-based care.

Hospitals, too, respond to incentives. In New York, for example, payers used to pay an all-inclusive daily rate. But a hospital's costs decline over a given patient's stay. The "tail end" days tend to cost less than the initial days because tests and treatments are often done soon after admission. As a result, New York hospitals found additional days quite profitable, and in the 1970s, New York had one of the longest lengths of stay in the country!

A similar story can be told about New Jersey, which pioneered the system for hospital payments now used by Medicare, the so-called DRG system. DRG stands for "Diagnostic Related Groups." The system sorts all admissions into one of several hundred categories. Then it pays the hospital a fixed fee for each admission in that category (with some special exceptions for "outlier" cases).

Economists had long predicted the results of such a scheme. Pay by the admission, instead of by the day, and admissions would rise and lengths of stay would fall. And that is exactly what happened in New Jersey!

The scheme was eventually adopted for Medicare nationally in 1983, as part of the so-called "Prospective Payment System," or PPS. Other payers have since also gone to this system, including some insurance companies and some state Medicaid systems. But different sources of payment still vary greatly in their generosity, which means that a hospital's "payer mix" greatly influences its financial circumstances.

There were many details to be worked out in actually using the DRG system, particularly the specific rates for each DRG. This was tricky because if a rate significantly exceeds the cost of caring for a specific type of case, hospitals will have a great incentive to seek out that kind of business. And this is apparently exactly what has happened in the case of cardiac catheterization.

"Cardiac cath," as it is called, is a very high-tech procedure in which a thin tube (a "cardiac catheter") is inserted in an artery in the leg. The tube is then threaded back through the circulatory system to the heart. This allows various contrast mediums to be introduced into the bloodstream, and hence detailed X-ray images to be made of the heart and its associated blood vessels. This is an essential step prior to cardiac surgery.

Given the generous reimbursement rate for this procedure, hospitals have been fighting to open such facilities. And given clinical ambiguity, when "cath labs" are opened, they can greatly increase the rate at which such procedures are done. There are documented cases in both Maine and New Hampshire where a given area's rate of catheterization increased radically when the local hospital added this service. Not only are such possibly unnecessary or inappropriate studies costly, but the complication rate for such procedures can exceed 1 percent.

Medicare also developed special financial allowances for teaching hospitals—hospitals that, as we will see shortly, tend to have especially high costs. These took several forms. Medicare not only paid for some of the direct costs of teaching, but Congress also added in an extra allowance for indirect teaching costs. Between these two, hospitals now collect more than $75,000 per resident per year (the majority from the congressional indirect adjustment). In addition, there was an adjustment for those hospitals with an especially large share of Medicaid recipients, which many teaching hospitals also have (the so-called "disproportionate share" adjustment).

Given all of these, many of the largest academic medical centers did very well in the 1980s, as the widespread wave of construction by such hospitals attests. One detailed study in Boston revealed that the major teaching hospitals built $2.2 billion worth of new facilities and still managed to add more than $1 billion to their cash reserves during this period.

If You Build It, We Will Pay

There was one other peculiarity of Medicare reimbursement that until recently has played a major role in fueling the hospital construction boom. Understanding this requires us to discuss a somewhat technical detail—similar to looking at an especially interesting bug down among the roots of the health care swamp—but it is worth the effort. The DRG system covered only operating costs, not capital costs. For the latter, Medicare reimbursed its share of a hospital's costs. Moreover, the "costs" they paid for included interest and depreciation, including depreciation on any assets built with donated funds.

Now, suppose a hospital borrowed to build some new facilities and arranged to pay off the loan like an ordinary home mortgage.

Payments in the early years would mainly be interest. This meant that the interest plus depreciation a hospital collected (at least on the Medicare portion—and often from Blue Cross as well) could significantly exceed its actual cash outlay, which involved lots of interest but only a small payment to principal.

Under this scheme depreciation payments could become a major source of hospital cash. Hence one way for a hospital to acquire cash was to build. And many shrewd hospital administrators did just that—despite the fact that there already was excess capacity in many areas. Perversely then, the reimbursement system provided the most capital to hospitals with the newest and most expensive facilities. Eventually, as principal payments increased and interest payments decreased, the revenue from reimbursement would be less than the hospital's cash outflow. But then the hospital could (and often did) either refinance its loan, or build another building. And unless the state had controls on hospital construction (controls which have become weaker and less prevalent in recent years), all this could occur without any real government review of the relative need for such investment.

One other result of this complex payment system has been to thoroughly confuse most consumers when it comes to understanding their hospital bills and health insurance paperwork. I have more than once been personally baffled by receiving in the mail something from a hospital that looked like a bill, that said I owed, say, $234.43, and that also had stamped prominently on it "This Is Not a Bill." When my insurance company, months later, denied payment for some piece of it, it then turned out it was a bill after all! On top of this, over 90 percent of all hospital bills have been found to contain errors.

In response, a whole industry has grown up to help individuals with their insurance claims, including specialized firms that deal with Medicare Part B. I was told about the latter by the retired chief operating officer of one of New York City's largest hospitals. He had become a satisfied client of one of these firms, after he, with all his experience, had found the task of filling out his own forms too confusing and overwhelming. Similarly, I know of a hospital in a medium-sized Midwestern city that has created a special volunteer group of local accountants to help elderly patients understand their bills. (This service is available to those enrolled in a special hospital program, equivalent to a frequent flyer program, which also includes complimentary valet parking.)

To summarize, money matters. On average, the doctors I know are probably more idealistic and committed than the members of most other professional groups. But to grow and prosper in difficult times they and their hospitals need revenue. So they are increasingly forced to respond to the signals we send to them through the marketplace, and to do what we pay them to do.

The U.S. Hospital System: Doing Well by Doing Good

There are something over 5,400 acute care community general hospitals in the United States, which are what we normally think of when we use the term hospital. In addition, there are some 880 specialty hospitals and 300-some-odd federal facilities. These range in size from less than 20 to more than 1,000 beds. And while 60 percent are not-for-profit entities, 26 percent are operated by local governments and 14 percent are owned by for-profit corporations. Some are parts of larger chains and some are operated by religious orders. Obviously these organizations vary enormously in structure, activities, financing, and so on.

Most hospitals do have some features in common. First, they are essentially *retail* operations. Customers will travel about as far to buy new clothes as they will for most hospital care—farther for a suit than a T-shirt and farther for heart surgery than a diagnostic X-ray. Still, the markets are surprisingly similar.

Thus the same forces that have disadvantaged many stores in older urban and suburban downtown areas have had a similar effect on hospitals. The suburban middle class does not want to fight downtown traffic, poor parking, and a feeling that the neighborhood is dangerous—either to shop or to seek medical care. Moreover, today nearly half of all hospital admissions come from the emergency room, and folks do not tend to drive far for that service. In addition, in 1992 more than half of all hospital surgery was done on an "outpatient" basis, which means without an overnight stay. Again, why travel far for such a short visit?

It's not surprising therefore that when the Lahey Clinic decided a decade ago to move from downtown Boston, it built its new facility directly adjacent to one of the area's largest shopping centers. The new building is on the ring road around Boston (Route 128) right next to the Burlington Mall.

In response, downtown hospitals are now seeking to cooperate with or acquire suburban facilities (or even open their own) in order to gain access to the now-moved-away patient population. This is especially so since suburban patients are more likely to be privately insured and thus pay more than those on Medicare or Medicaid. For example, Henry Ford Hospital in Detroit has put together a whole system of satellite community hospitals and outpatient clinics. Similarly, most of the major heart surgery teams from the downtown Chicago teaching hospitals now also operate, some days a week, in selected suburban locations.

But if hospitals are largely not-for-profit institutions, why do they respond to market incentives so assiduously? Partly this is because of the financial pressure exerted by an ever-tighter reimbursement system. Managers, unsure about future government policy, feel it is only prudent to secure their hospital's financial position. Many institutions have therefore felt that they had no choice but to seek out new ways to acquire revenue. Quite a few have created various for-profit and not-for-profit subsidiaries, as part of a wave of corporate restructuring. These various entities not only undertake medical functions (such as doing laboratory work for others or operating a nursing home), but also engage in entrepreneurial ventures like hotels or retirement communities.

But the current pattern of hospital behavior is not just a response to the external world. It also reflects institutional structures and incentives, and the personal interests of those involved. *To say that an organization is not-for-profit does not mean that it makes no profit.* Rather, it means that there is no external group—i.e., no shareholders—who have a claim to those profits. Instead, all the profits remain within the organization and can be, and are, used to further its growth. Such organizations are also exempt from state and federal corporate income taxes on those profits, which makes their accumulation even easier.

The original theory behind not-for-profit hospitals was the "Robin Hood" approach: make money from the rich and use it to provide care for the poor. But as the cost of caring for the poor has increased, and the rich try to limit what they pay, this strategy has become increasingly problematic. Instead, administrators, trustees, doctors (and even patients), have increasingly come to operate as if the relevant motto for hospital management was the Samuel Gompers principal. Gompers, the first president of the American Federation of Labor, was once asked, "Mr. Gompers, what exactly is it you want for the American worker?" Gompers replied, "More!"

A successful hospital building campaign appears to benefit everyone. Trustees enjoy added prestige, doctors and patients get new facilities, and hospital managers receive the sort of recognition that might allow them to move up to a better job. No wonder American hospitals have occupancy rates in the 60 percent range and yet continue to build. Not only do we have excess capacity, but in many areas our hospital buildings are very new—so aggressively have we invested.

Those who pay the bill have reason for concern—yet their capacity to restrain the providers is limited. As we saw in previous chapters, business and government have much else to do, and consumers have little in the way of incentives (or capacity) to organize for the seemingly silly goal of denying themselves better service. Indeed, as long as most consumers don't pay any more for going to a fancy new building than to a slightly aging facility, all things being equal, they will tend to choose the newer option. At least that is what most hospital administrators claim to believe. The result, in many cities, has been a medical facilities arms race.

The dynamics of hospital expansion have also been influenced by hospitals' internal organizational structure. That structure makes hospitals what may be the most unmanageable organizations in America. In a way, community hospitals are like the saber-toothed tiger—a highly specialized beast that can survive only in a suitably accommodating environment. Sabertooths had such unwieldy teeth that they could kill only one kind of prey: the giant ground sloth. When they became such efficient predators that the sloths were all killed off, the saber-tooth also disappeared!

Critical to this unmanageability is the peculiar relationship, in most hospitals, between the hospital and the doctor. Doctors, after all, control most of the major production decisions in the institution. They decide who gets what tests, procedures, medications, or surgery. And yet doctors have only the most tenuous organizational connection to the hospital itself. And under the current reimbursement system, hospitals have every incentive to control certain kinds of utilization once a patient is admitted— while doctors generally have an incentive to do more.

The group of doctors who admits patients to a hospital constitutes its "medical staff." They typically decide who else can join, formulate rules about staff conduct, and negotiate with the administration over how they are to be treated. But they are *not* hospital employees. There are a few doctors, like radiologists and pathologists (who run X-ray and laboratory services) who are different. Such hospital-based physicians often have some sort of revenue-sharing relationship with the hospital, or might even be on salary. But the majority of the medical staff function as independent "crafts people" who use the hospital as a "workshop"—and use it free of charge.

Since the hospitals depend on admissions, they have to be attractive to doctors in order to survive. So hospitals woo doctors—with inexpensive staff parking, or conveniently located buildings for their private offices, or by acquiring the latest medical equipment. This helps explain why so many hospitals duplicate each other's services and equipment. Small rural hospitals often have the problem of getting doctors to locate in their service area to begin with. Aggressive recruiting efforts, various kinds of financial support, and other incentives are commonplace in such cases.

Not only is the medical staff outside the hospital administrator's control, but the rest of the organization is often structured in ways that are quite irrational from a production perspective. That is, hospitals tend to be organized "vertically" by professional or technical specialty, not "horizontally" around multidisciplinary teams caring for a group of patients. This can greatly complicate routine coordination and cooperation. Problems have to go up and then down these various hierarchies because no one is in charge of all the inputs involved in providing care to a given patient. For example, suppose a nurse on a floor is having trouble getting the housekeepers to clean attentively. In many places the nurse has to go to the unit manager, who goes to a supervisor, who goes to the vice president for nursing, who goes across to the vice president for operations, who goes down to the head of housekeeping, etc., etc.

These problems become even more difficult in the large teaching hospitals that are connected to major medical schools (of which there are perhaps 300 in the country). In such academic medical centers there will often be both faculty members on staff who treat patients and some community physicians who have admitting privileges. The faculty tend to be focused on academic concerns, on teaching and research. And yet their incomes will often depend in part on the volume of their clinical practice. So both they and the administration must juggle conflicting priorities. Moreover, with many very sick patients, such hospitals utilize a daunting array of technical specialists. Hence the number of distinct "vertical" units multiplies. Then there are all the residents, the medical students, and the medical school administration to deal with. Indeed, in a complex medical center, there might also be a nursing school, training programs for other technical specialists like occupational therapists or X-ray technicians, and perhaps satellite clinics or specialized subsidiaries as well.

As a result of all this complexity, teaching hospitals are typically far more expensive—perhaps twice as expensive—as ordinary community hospitals. Some of this is due to the need for stand-by capacity to deal with complex cases. But much of the difference is due to the costs of paying for the people doing teaching and research, and the managerial complexity these activities produce. Yes, those involved in teaching also do provide significant patient care. But by their very nature teaching hospitals require both faculty and residents that community hospitals do not have to support. And these additional bodies all have to get paid, and they have to be administratively supported, and the tests they order have to be performed.

The managerial structure required to guide a hospital with multiple missions and many relationships also expands significantly. Such hospitals now have elaborate strategic planning and contract management functions, marketing executives and public relations people, financial analysts, and internal quality managers. Moreover, many of these individuals are well paid. And they have secretaries and assistants and computers and telephones and copying machines and fancy offices. And these costs too are supported by patient care dollars.

At the opposite end of the scale from the major teaching hospitals are rural hospitals and the community hospitals in small towns. These institutions have found the going especially tough recently. The DRG reimbursement system has led to shorter lengths of stay. And insurance company efforts to control care have led to fewer admissions. Increasingly, less complicated surgery is being done on an outpatient basis and those with less complicated medical conditions are often no longer admitted at all. Yet these less serious cases were often exactly what smaller hospitals primarily handled—so they find themselves in the declining part of the market. At the same time, the growing parts of the market are in the "hi-tech" areas like cardiac surgery.

As a result of all these trends, more and more patients from small towns and rural areas are going to the major medical centers for the diminishing volume of hospital care they receive—because they go for only the most serious conditions. In many states, therefore, a good number of smaller and more rural hospitals have been forced to close in recent years. And more are likely to do so.

Also worth a special mention are the nation's public hospitals, especially those in the larger cities. Hospital emergency rooms have a legal obligation to treat everyone in need of care. Yet in practice, especially for non-emergency cases, often only the public hospital really welcomes everyone—including the uninsured, the socially marginal, the undocumented, and so on. Indeed before the rules were tightened up, more prestigious hospitals had been known to "turf" the uninsured to public institutions—that is, to send non-fully-recovered patients over to the public hospital. Another tactic to avoid nonpaying patients has been for hospitals to close their trauma services. This allows them to avoid the expensive and often uninsured patients such services generate—leaving this "business" also to the public hospitals. The resulting decrease in accessibility can in turn create problems—as the decline in trauma centers in downtown Los Angeles illustrates.

In many jurisdictions, public hospitals have become such a fiscal drain on the city that they have been closed (as in Philadelphia) or "spun off" into free-standing corporations (as in Memphis, Tennessee). Exactly what role they will play in any reformed health care system is unclear. Yet some way will have to be found to keep them functioning if access for the disadvantaged is to be preserved.

The problems of managing a hospital also force us to focus on the absolutely critical role of nursing in the process of hospital care. Nurses are the single largest occupation group in any hospital and they are the individuals who actually do the bulk of the patient care. Yet at various times in recent years, the growth in demand for nurses has outstripped the supply, and hospitals have faced serious shortages.

The widespread impression that the shortages have been caused by nurses leaving the profession for other lines of work turns out not to have been the case. In fact, the number of employed nurses, both absolutely and in relation to the population, has continued to grow through various labor market cycles over the last twenty years. But demand has periodically increased even faster—especially with the growth of so-called "intensive-care units" that use at least four times as many nurses per bed as regular hospital floors.

The way hospitals have responded to periodic nursing shortages reveals many of the faults of traditional hospital management. Throughout the 1970s and 1980s, the demographics of the nursing work force were steadily changing. Many were entering nursing later in life—the mean age of new RNs is now about thirty—and so more and more nurses are individuals with families. Yet for years hospitals persisted in rigid three-shift schedules, often requiring less senior nurses to rotate among day and evening, or night shifts. Rather than pay extra for night or weekend work, they relied on traditional ideas of "equal sacrifice" that imposed great burdens on some of their employees. In part, this was a reflection of the lack of management training among many hospital (and nursing) managers. The notion that one should tailor compensation and scheduling to fit the needs of the work force has now become widely accepted—but it took a long time to do so.

Adapting to a Changing Ecology

Increasingly, all hospital administrators, including nursing managers, have management training. As one major hospital CEO put it, "We used to tell people 'Don't worry, you'll learn'— but that is no longer enough." As a result, these institutions have become steadily more "businesslike." The service vision and the charitable impulse that traditionally provided an organizational mission have become less prominent. A new managerial generation of bright young folks with desktop computers has swept into place with a keen "bottom line" orientation. This was put in sharp relief for me by a nonphysician administrator who ran a for-profit company that provided kidney dialysis for those covered by the ESRD program. He once said to me, "I'll dialyze a telephone post if it's Medicare eligible!"

Some of the results of this transformation are highly desirable. Many hospitals now have excellent data systems, flexible and imaginative scheduling and compensation plans for employees, and sophisticated financial management practices. But there is another side to all this.

The trend toward business management practices has now progressed so far that the one-time controversy over for-profit versus not-for-profit hospitals is no longer very relevant. Critics once claimed that for-profit institutions did not share the "essential spirit" of the hospital. But now, as almost every institution diversifies, reorganizes, forms alliances, and seeks new markets, it seems as if all hospitals operate in the for-profit, revenue-maximizing mode. The chief executives of large nonprofit teaching hospitals are even compensated like the managers of major for-profit companies—that is, in the $500,000 to $1 million a year range.

The new attitude of entrepreneurship reminds one a bit of the chorus in a song by the 1960s satirist Tom Lehrer. He wrote about Wernher von Braun, head of the U.S. moon rocket program, who had supervised work on the German V-2 rockets aimed at England during World War II. The chorus is as follows: " 'Once the rockets are up, who cares where they come down? That's not my department,' says Wernher von Braun."

In part, the complexity of the U.S. reimbursement system is to blame for the high administrative costs characteristic of American institutions. Each public and private insurance scheme has its own forms and processes. And the hospital has to deal with all of them. Insurance companies all attempt to limit the care their policyholders receive. So the hospital maintains its own staff to fight with, and justify, its decisions to the various payers. Providing that justification also leads to an enormous amount of record keeping, not to mention substantial daily aggravation. Hospital administrators in Boston joke that all their decisions seem to require the approval of one anonymous, relatively junior insurance company employee located at the other end of a telephone line—whom they imagine sitting in a windowless cubicle in some low-wage area like Utah or South Dakota.

Regulation also exacerbates that administrative burden. Hospitals are under the jurisdiction of a large number of different agencies: city, county, and state health departments, various federal agencies, and various private sector accrediting organizations, including JCAHO (pronounced "Jay-Co": the Joint Commission on Accreditation of Healthcare Organizations). The multiplicity and pettiness of the resulting rules—even when they are well motivated—can be trying to the most conscientious hospital manager.

For example, JCAHO has recently become concerned that the amount of equipment often stored in hospital corridors might hinder mobility in an emergency. At least one hospital, with no other place to store such material, had several moving vans of "stuff" driven around the city for the day JCAHO visited. That was the only way its corridors could meet what the managers thought was an unrealistic rule.

Yet for all of this managerial attention, and all the talk of competition, hospitals' concerns with "customer service" remains uneven. Many hospitals have started "guest relations" programs to involve and motivate employees to be more responsive to patients and families. Yet clinical staff have been known to respond with either cynicism (about "smile school") or hostility. At one Arizona hospital, the surgeons attended such a training session wearing stickers that said "Lawyers and hookers have customers and clients. Doctors have patients."

Still, there has been a significant advance in management attention to these issues. There are now several national programs which foster quality management and patient-centered care. And various survey instruments have been developed to allow hospitals to monitor patient experience, and in some cases to give patients information on hospital performance.

One area where such shopping is particularly evident is in baby delivery. Those who will need this procedure know far enough in advance to stop and plan. And many customers have their own views about how they want to proceed. As a result of shifting social attitudes, many variations in patterns of practice have developed—natural childbirth, baby "rooming-in" with mother, family members in the delivery room, homelike delivery rooms, and so on. Moreover, the catalyst for all of this has typically been the customers. I know of one hospital that heralded the opening of its new maternity service with an aggressive advertising campaign modeled on Burger King. While it didn't say so explicitly, the clear message of the inserts it put into weekly suburban newspapers was "Have it your way." Whether such experience is an applicable or desirable model for future hospital competition is something we return to below.

The Joys of Creative Accounting

Before we leave our discussion of hospitals, we need to once again look at some relatively narrow details of the swamp's ecology. In fact, what we now seek is an elusive, perhaps mythical swamp beast: namely, a hospital's "real" profit level.

Hospital accounting is done by the "accrual" method. Charges for expenses are made against a hospital's revenue not when the money flows out but when accounting standards say it is appropriate to do so because the "costs" in question are "associated" with the year's activities. By overstating such charges—and putting the money into various reserve funds—a hospital can alter the profit rate it reports to the public. In addition, many possibilities are opened up by having the hospital be a part of a larger complex of organizational entities. Funds can now be "parked" with various affiliated corporations or foundations. Given such possibilities, it can be quite difficult to evaluate

a hospital's financial status without a sophisticated analysis—
including a look at the accounts of the various affiliated entities
and corporations.

The reasons to undertake "creative accounting" are not hard
to find. Hospitals that did well financially during the 1980s did
not necessarily want to make it clear how well they had done.
High reported profits might hurt charitable contributions or provoke demands for lower rates or for more community service.
Indeed, last year in Boston a report that revealed just how much
those hospitals had earned led to exactly that debate.

Another equally elusive swamp dweller is the "cost" of any
given hospital service. This creature is not only hard to see, but
different observers give totally different accounts of its size and
appearance. Hospitals typically quote what accountants call "fully
allocated average cost." This number is developed by taking all
the capital costs, central administrative expenses, and the cost of
all support services in the hospital and "allocating" these to the
various revenue-producing units. In this way all costs are shown
as the cost of some activity that generates revenue.

There are obviously many different ways such an allocation
might be done, although Medicare does have a standard format
that moderately limits such discretion, and hospitals generally use
that. Still the allocation rules themselves have been influenced by
hospitals' desire to maximize revenue.

Consider the following example. Traditionally some payers
reimbursed hospitals more generously for ER costs than for
inpatient costs. As a result, the rules for allocating overhead were
often developed to make ER "costs" as large as possible. For
example, each outpatient visit and each inpatient admission were
considered as equivalent units of activity when it came to allocating medical records costs. In fact an admission typically generates
much more of a burden on records than an outpatient visit, but
this rule served to shift costs to the outpatient side.

As a result of all these intricacies, a substantial amount of
overhead expense is typically "loaded" onto the emergency
room. This explains how the basic "cost" for the cheapest
emergency room visit can be over $150. Such figures include a
fraction of the cost of the CEO's salary, a piece of the interest on
the bonds for the new parking garage, and so on.

Fully allocated costs do not tell us what it would actually cost (or save) the hospital if it did a little more or a little less of a given procedure or service. For example, what would actually happen to ER costs if a few folks more or less were served? Depending on how big an adjustment in volume is being considered, such "incremental" costs could be anywhere from 10 to 60 percent of the kinds of costs usually quoted.

Now that we understand what "fully allocated average costs" really means, we can reconsider the whole question of "cost shifting." Private insurance companies, which pay such costs, or even charges, feel they are cross-subsidizing publicly financed patients who pay less. From a purely economic viewpoint, there is no reason why different payers should necessarily pay the same price. Deciding how an enterprise sets its prices, to cover all its fixed costs, is appropriately a strategic managerial decision. And there is no reason why such a decision has to be constrained by one particular set of formal accounting rules.

Nonetheless, someone has to pay for all the costs of the hospital. And to the extent that the public sector is relying on its purchasing power to shift costs to private payers, the latter are understandably aggravated.

Indeed the individuals who are often most victimized by these practices are the honest uninsured who can wind up paying the most for care. For example, when such patients utilize the emergency room, they confront a price that reflects a significant markup, even over fully allocated average costs. Most insurers, in contrast, have negotiated much more favorable rates. This only encourages hospitals to raise their nominal prices even further, exactly because so few actually pay them, to the disadvantage of those few who do.

This difference between average and incremental costs, which some hospitals have recently focused on, also explains why many institutions have begun to actively seek out Medicare patients (and in some areas even Medicaid patients as well), despite the calculated "shortfall." Government reimbursement rates may be less than fully allocated average costs, but, at the same time, they are also often greater than the actual incremental costs of caring for such patients. So the hospital actually makes money by treating such additional cases—compared with the alternative of leaving the beds empty.

Why have I gone into such detail on these aspects of hospital structure and behavior? Hospitals, after all, are the single biggest segment of the health care system—about 40 percent of total health expenditures. Moreover, that number understates their real role. Many other costs and incomes that are generated in the hospital are not counted as hospital costs, such as all the bills physicians send out separately for services performed on patients in the hospital.

More important, the internal complexity of hospitals helps suggest why health care cost containment is so difficult. Their weak and divided internal structures make it difficult for even very good managers to exercise effective control. Yet these are highly evolved institutions, with many connections to their communities. And since internal change will be so difficult for them, their first response will be to try to continue to do what they have been doing. They will try to find new ways to generate revenues to keep all those internal pressure groups happy. But the health care world is changing and hospitals, even those most legitimately pleased with their own past accomplishments, are going to have to change with it. It is not that we have to tame the saber-tooths. Instead we will have to both help and persuade them to evolve in ways that they might find painful. And that will not be an easy task for anyone.

Training and Paying for Marcus Welby

Two features of the American system of medical education have contributed significantly to the current health care crisis: the cost of that education and the values that it communicates to physicians-in-training. The United States and Canada are the only industrialized countries in the world that require students to have an undergraduate degree before going on to medical school, and the U.S. is the only one where most of medical education is *not* government financed.

The total financial burden of medical training now can be quite staggering. If we consider tuition and room and board costs for four years at a private college and then four years at a private medical school, the sum could now run to $200,000! Even a student who goes to a state school could spend in the vicinity of $100,000 when living costs are considered. Another real cost of medical education is the income doctors forego, not only when in school, but also during their "postgraduate medical education." During this period, of from one to five years, doctors serve as residents in teaching hospitals, caring for patients under the ever-decreasing supervision of senior physicians. Pay for residents is often typically low—$25,000 to $35,000—too low to allow young physicians who have accumulated substantial debts to do much about beginning to pay them off.

So now we have young men and women, in their late twenties or early thirties, embarking on medical practice with debts that often range from $25,000 to $75,000 or even more. Is it any wonder that their decisions are influenced by their sense of economic vulnerability and prior financial deprivation? Perhaps for these reasons, American physicians' salaries now average nearly $200,000 per year. This is more than the compensation of physicians in most other countries—and a higher multiple of average wages than what physicians earn in those other countries.

It is also not surprising that America now trains relatively few general practitioners or family physicians—whose earnings tend to be less than other specialists. Nor should we be surprised that few doctors want to practice in poor rural areas or decaying inner cities, where they can anticipate lower incomes. Young doctors also want to live where there are good schools for their children, compatible colleagues, well-equipped hospitals, and cultural opportunities. For those who do not come from rural areas, such a life can seem unattractive. And even for those who do, there is always the problem of "How You Gonna Keep 'Em Down on the Farm After They've Seen Paree?" As a result, a higher-than-usual percentage of the doctors in such areas are from foreign countries. Apparently they feel they are at less of a competitive disadvantage in regions where there are fewer other physicians.

It is also relevant to consider the values young physicians-in-training acquire during their education. Medical school faculty—whom students naturally emulate—are themselves highly specialized. In part this is a rational response to the explosion of medical knowledge. "Being the best," or "being on the frontier," increasingly requires adopting a narrow focus. But the system develops a logic of its own, and during medical school everyone wants to see an unusual or "interesting" case. Highly intellectually competitive, medical students are excited by such challenges. And training in a major medical center provides such experience. As one medical educator jokes, eight years in an academic medical center teaches young doctors the following decision rule: "When you hear hoofbeats, think zebras!"

I once experienced this quite directly. My second child, at age two, suddenly developed an infection that swelled the whole side of her face and head. Admitted to Children's Hospital in Boston, she was seen by more than thirty-five residents and staff doctors in the first four hours. Word spread quickly that there was an interesting case! No one knew what was going on. She was put on a broad spectrum antibiotic. The swelling went down and later that evening, a first-year resident in pediatric dentistry spotted the infected cut on the inside of her mouth that was apparently the culprit. Then we remembered; she had been chewing on an old clam shell the previous day! Thereafter, few but her own doctor came to see her.

Various selection and socialization processes begin to shape young physicians well before medical school ever begins. The students who are admitted are not necessarily those who have the best interpersonal skills. Most of the required courses in a "premed" curriculum are in science, and highly challenging. One result is that the "premed grind," obsessed with grades, has become a well-developed stereotype in contemporary popular culture.

Of course many doctors are motivated to do good as they understand it. That is why they went to medical school in the first place. And many are motivated by a sense of intellectual excitement, their own skill, or a personal commitment to choose this or that special field. Primary care does have its drawbacks. Dispensing penicillin for an eight-year-old's strep throat doesn't seem to everyone like the best way to make use of all that struggle and all that education. Still the balance of rewards we offer makes it harder, not easier, for those who do have a sense of mission—which seems a bit backward from a social policy perspective.

Personality and background also enter into such choices. takes a different kind of person to be a surgeon than to be a psychiatrist. And several studies confirm that to some extent doctors sort themselves among specialties in ways that make psychological sense. After all, pathologists, who work in laboratories, don't need the same "people skills" as, say, a family physician.

This pattern also manifests itself in the political orientations of various medical specialty groups. The American Academy of Pediatrics, for example, tends to be much more liberal than the American College of Surgeons. This will affect the politics of health care reform. The medical community will not speak with a single voice. For example, there is a physicians' group called the American College of Physicians. Many of these individuals are general internists (as opposed to subspecialists) who have decided to undertake this form of practice as a way to pursue the goal of being an all-around doctor in the modern world of high-tech medicine. Many of them thus have a reformist orientation, and their organization has endorsed a relatively radical plan for health care reform.

Another major factor transforming American medicine has been the increased role of women, who now constitute about one-half of the first-year medical school class. To be sure, women physicians vary as much in their views and attitudes as do their male counterparts, and one must be as aware of stereotyping female physicians as of stereotyping any other group. Still many young women physicians have gone into specialties like obstetrics or pediatrics. They also seem somewhat more willing than men have been to work in group practice settings, or on salary in HMOs. And this in turn has made it easier for those organizations to recruit the staff they need.

In summary, American doctors are a varied lot. They range from medical school faculty subspecialists concerned with their research and publication to community physicians concerned with building a practice and developing a reputation for responding to patient needs. Yet all of them have to decide how to respond to the financial incentives they face, given the years and dollars that they have invested in their own training.

Many of them are also increasingly unhappy. Some recent

that the current practice environment makes as
ercent of practicing physicians wish that they had
medical career. The demands of insurance compa-
its on professional discretion, the paperwork, the
hassie, lower incomes, and diminished community respect
have demoralized many of them. Yet they are vital not only to
the care of patients, but also to the future of health care reform.
Their political power may have diminished in recent years but
should not be underrated. Can the reformers offer the doctors
something that will elicit their cooperation, or at least blunt their
opposition? That is an issue we will have to consider further in
the next chapter as we look at various reform options.

Where Are We?

Where does all this leave us? Again, a well-known maxim is
in order. As that most famous of all American swamp dwellers,
Pogo (an opossum, by the way), once put it, "We have met the
enemy and they is us."

The system we live with is one we have created. The insurance companies, public programs, hospitals, and medical schools
in the United States are *not* the work of God or nature.

But because many individuals have invested their whole lives
in current arrangements, the system has a substantial capacity for
self-preservation. It will respond to incentives more than it will to
exhortation, in part because we have pushed it to evolve in that
way. On the other hand, the very variety, complexity, and scale
of America may help make change possible. Not all hospitals are
the same and not all doctors have the same values and interests.
Still, a very substantial act of political will will be required to
produce change.

When it comes to predicting the impact of various health care
reforms, wishing will not make it so. A clear-eyed, even slightly
cynical view of the system will be required if we are to be able to
proceed sensibly. But before we can get to the plans, a bit of a
pause and some systematic stock-taking are in order. Now that
we know so much about the system—its structure, functioning,
funding and so on—what are we actually getting for all this? How
are we doing?

TAKING STOCK:
The Results of the American
Health Care System

Relative to What?

After our somewhat exhausting trip through the health care
swamp, the time has come to evaluate the performance of the
system we have explored. The problem of doing so was well
posed in a famous line by the old-time New York comedian
Henny Youngman. "I was walking down the street the other day
and I met a friend of mine. This friend said to me, 'Henny, how's
your wife?' and I said, 'Relative to what?' "

One way for us to make relevant comparisons is to look at
the experience of other industrialized countries. How much do
various nations spend, and what do they get for that spending
both in terms of health care services and ultimate health outcomes? Obviously nations do differ significantly in culture and
expectations, in the extent of their social problems, and in their
demographic patterns. Still, employed with appropriate caution,
an international perspective can help us see how our health care
system is performing.

The analysis that follows draws on data published by the Organization for Economic Cooperation and Development (the OECD) for all Western European nations, the United States, Canada, Australia, New Zealand, and Japan. In order to make the most relevant comparisons abroad, Spain, Portugal, Ireland, Greece, and Turkey are generally excluded from the analysis. The most recent available data are from 1991, and all expenditures have been converted into U.S. dollars in a way that adjusts for differences in purchasing power among nations. The base the OECD uses for such comparisons is Gross Domestic Product or GDP. (This number differs only marginally from the figure more familiar in the United States, Gross National Product or GNP.)

"Bottom Lines": Money and Lives

Before looking at the actual numbers. I want to state what I believe is the central paradox revealed by the quite voluminous data. *The United States spends a great deal more than any other advanced industrial country on health care and yet gets no more in terms of health outcomes or health care services, and in many cases less, for that spending.* The bulk of this chapter will be devoted to understanding this paradox. But first, this claim seems so surprising and implausible, and yet also so important in shaping our attitudes toward health care reform, that a detailed look at the data seems in order.

How much *do* we spend? The most relevant comparison, if we want to relate spending to outcomes, is simply to look at per capita expenditures. Per capita costs are also important from the viewpoint of international competitiveness because these are what determine health care costs per worker.

What we find is a *big* difference! In 1991, the United States spent $2,868 per capita, Canada spent $1,915, Germany $1,659 and Japan $1,307. All the rest of the advanced industrial world spent amounts between Canada and Japan, except for Denmark, Britain, and New Zealand, which were *lower* still.

Let's pause for a minute and reflect on what these numbers mean. The United States is spending more than *twice* as much per capita on health care as many of our major industrial competitors. Even Canada, the country most like the United States in geography, climate, history, and ethnicity, spends less than two thirds of what we spend. Nor is this result a statistical artifact. If anything the European data tend to overstate their costs, by counting some expenditures as health care that are not included in that total by the United States.

A defender of the U.S. health care system is ready with a counterattack. Now, wait a minute, he cries, perhaps this disparity is due to the fact that the United States is so much richer than other countries. We spend more because we have more to spend. That must be it! Therefore we should not look at *absolute* spending but at the *share* of the economy devoted to health care. Isn't that the calculation that shows us how much of a burden health care is placing on the rest of the economy?

Well, percentages don't in fact tell us about cost per worker, but still they are interesting—so let's look at those too. In fact, in 1991, the United States was the highest-spending nation by a noticeable margin, with 13.2 percent of its economy as measured by GDP devoted to health care. (Current estimates are that in 1993 we will spend over 14 percent.) The next highest advanced industrial country was Canada at 10 percent. The United Kingdom, Denmark, and Japan were again at the bottom, at a bit over 6 percent—or again half of our spending even on a percentage basis. The rest of our comparison nations spent in the 7 to 9 percent range. Clearly health care does impose a bigger burden, relatively as well as absolutely, on the United States than it does on the economies of any of our major competitors.

It is true that if the U.S. economy were doing better, our output would be higher, and so for any given level of health care expenditures, the percentage of GDP devoted to health care would be lower. But that observation only illustrates the important fact that health care costs have been increasing at a rate that does not seem determined by external economic forces, but rather by the system's internal dynamics.

Well, our American enthusiast replies, the problem with using simple percentages is that it is not a sophisticated enough analysis. Health care is what economists call a "luxury good"—and so spending on health care grows faster than income when income grows. So we would expect even the share of an economy devoted to health care to increase with economic growth. Doesn't that explain U.S. spending?

To test that claim, we need to look at the relationship, across countries, between per capita GDP and per capita health expenditures. We can do this by constructing a statistical trend line, using the OECD sample, to summarize that relationship. When we do that we find a good "fit" to the data. Most countries experience clusters very tightly about such a trend line, and the relationship itself is surprisingly stable, not having changed significantly between 1980 and 1991.

Yet even here the United States is different from other countries. We actually spend noticeably more on health care than our per capita GDP would lead one to expect given the international pattern. Moreover, during the 1980s our spending got steadily further out of line. In 1980 we spent $150 dollars per capita per year more on health than one would have expected. By 1991 that had risen to nearly $1,000.

A final fiscal comparison focuses on rates of growth in health care expenditure. Such an analysis says something about the capacity of a country to control its health care costs. Here again the United States leads the world. Our rate of growth of 9 percent annually from 1985 through 1991 leads experts to project that health care could increase to 20 percent of GDP by the year 2010—only 15 years away! In Germany, in contrast, health spending has grown at the same rate as GDP, so that the share of GDP devoted to health (a bit over 8 percent) is the same as it was twenty years ago.

Since we spend so much more than everyone else—between 50 percent and 100 percent per capita—what exactly are we getting for it? The response suggested by the data completes the paradox. The disappointing answer is, apparently not very much!

Let us begin with the most obvious outcome measure, life expectancy. Here Japan leads the way, with a life expectancy at birth of seventy-six years for males and eighty-two for females. The United States lags at seventy-two for males and seventy-nine for females. For those not familiar with such data, let me assure you, three or four years of life expectancy over the whole population is a *major* difference. For example, estimates suggest that curing cancer would add only two to three years to our national life expectancy. Moreover, the other advanced industrial countries, which spend *much less* than we do on their health care, tend to do the *same or better* than we do when it comes to life expectancy.

This result is so surprising that one is tempted to look for idiosyncratic explanations for it. In particular, is it due to international differences in violence or infant mortality? In fact, these do not account for the mediocre performance of the U.S. health care system. The U.S. homicide rate is ten times as high as Great Britain's and four times as high as Canada's. But we can largely eliminate the effect of that phenomena by looking at life expectancy at age sixty—which reflects differences in the effectiveness of a nation's acute health care system. Here, too, despite our higher spending, the United States does not do noticeably better, and in many cases somewhat worse, than the nations in our comparison group.

There are other factors which would actually lead us to expect *better* health outcomes in the United States. Smoking is much more prevalent in Europe and Japan than it is in America. And many European diets are even higher in fat than American diets. Blood cholesterol levels tend to be higher and obesity more prevalent in, say, Germany than in the United States. Since those over sixty-five use three times per capita more health care resources than individuals under age sixty-five, we might wonder if demographics could explain our high-risk spending. However, the populations of most European nations, on average, are actually *older* than ours. So, demographics cannot explain our paradox.

If infant mortality rates were very high and varied greatly among countries, they could distort these life expectancy measures. It took me years to understand how the Founding Fathers at the time of the American Revolution could all have been so old, when my junior high school history book said that life expectancy in America at that time was less than forty. In fact, what happened in those days was that so many died in childhood. As a result, the overall life expectancy figures did not reflect the life span of those who survived to become adults. But now infant mortality rates are too low in all industrial countries to significantly affect comparative life expectancy numbers.

Still infant mortality—which includes all deaths of those under one year of age—is considered by many to be one of the most sensitive barometers of the effectiveness of a nation's health care system. And, sad to say, among our comparison group, the United States has the worst infant mortality rate of all. Moreover, our relative position has declined noticeably. In 1960, Canada, France, Japan, and Germany all had infant mortality rates greater than ours—as did Austria, Belgium, Ireland, Italy, and Spain! Today all these nations' rates are below that of the United States—and Japan's rate is down to approximately half of ours.

Within the United States, these rates vary substantially by income, race, and education. The distinct effects of these factors are somewhat difficult to disentangle. What we do know is that despite an overall improvement for both groups, infant mortality rates among whites continue to be less than half of the rates among African-Americans. Moreover, much of this difference appears to be due to differences in the frequency of low-birth-weight babies between these two groups—which in turn has a major impact on what is called "neonatal mortality," infant deaths that occur in the first twenty-eight days. Indeed, a substantial part of our poor international performance seems related to our relatively high rate of low-birth-weight infants.

Comparing infant mortality rates is not always straightforward. This is worth noting because it signals just how cautious one has to be before jumping to even the most apparent statistical conclusion. Hospitals with aggressive neonatal intensive care units may get heartbeats and respiration started in more newborns, who then die. This elevates the hospital's apparent infant mortality rate (in which stillborns do not "count"). And such practices may be more common in the United States than in other countries. Because of this some experts advocate computing a "late fetal plus neonatal death rate" for comparative purposes. However, even when we do that, the relative position of the United States improves only slightly.

Many kinds of variation among populations can influence infant mortality. Recent data from Massachusetts reveal the following complex pattern. Compared to whites, African-Americans make less use of prenatal care and have a higher infant mortality rate. Asian-Americans make even less use of such care than

African-Americans and yet they have even better birth outcomes than do whites.

This result appears to reflect patterns of social and economic inequality that transcend health care—especially since low-birth-weight and neonatal mortality depend heavily on a mother's experience during pregnancy. Making progress on these obviously unjust disparities will therefore require social as well as medical programs, including efforts aimed at improving maternal nutrition, living conditions, and substance abuse.

Much of health care is not devoted to lifesaving but to improving individuals' quality of life. While data on life expectancy and infant mortality may not measure everything we want to measure—at least they are relatively objective. Measures of "quality of life" are much more difficult to construct and use because they require some clinical or philosophic framework for combining different kinds of disability and injury into a single scale. As we will see in Chapter 7, this exact problem has arisen in the course of Oregon's efforts to rank the benefits of various health care procedures. As we might expect, there is no social consensus on what those weights should be—since determining the relevant values is a social and political, not a scientific problem.

Despite all these statistical, practical, and philosophical difficulties, the central paradox of the U.S. health care system remains. How and why do we spend so much more and yet not seem to get that much more for it? Is our care so poor, our utilization so misguided, our system so inefficient? These are the questions to which we now turn.

The "Bestest" or Just the "Mostest"?

The notion that the high cost/modest gain paradox might be due to poor quality flies in the face of much of the popular and political rhetoric about American health care. Over and over we have been treated to the conclusion that America has "the best health care in the world." To explore this contention, and the relationship of quality to outcomes, we first need to define what we mean by quality—itself no easy task.

Quality is often confused with quantity, as when someone

says—"Grandma got the best care. They did everything possible for her." The problem with that definition can be seen by referring once more to the idea of "payoff functions." When we discussed these previously, they all had the form of the one in Figure 5. At some point, Z in the diagram, "diminishing marginal returns" set in so that additional resources don't result in any additional benefit. It is hard to argue that added resources beyond the "flat of the curve" really contribute to increased quality.

Even more dramatically, it is quite possible that the relevant payoff functions actually *turn down,* as in Figure 6. Thus beyond level X added spending actually makes the patient *worse off.* How could this be?

Additional health care can be harmful in several different circumstances. First, patients might undergo unnecessary surgery—which always has risks. Patients can also stay in hospitals too long for optimal recovery, because they don't get enough exercise. Moreover, the longer someone is in the hospital, the more they are at risk for infections. And hospital-acquired infections can be especially drug-resistant, since they are caused by bacteria that have evolved in response to the heavy treatment common in a hospital environment. Or patients may undergo too many tests and procedures they do not need, each of which has some risk of side effects or complications. When care makes patients actually worse off, we refer to such events as "iatrogenic" injury.

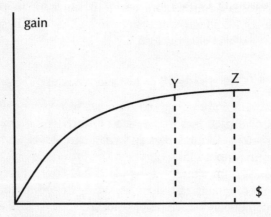

Figure 5

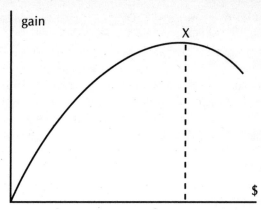

Figure 6

The first dimension of quality then is *appropriateness*. Do patients receive the right tests and treatments? This is a matter of both the amount that is done, and whether the right kinds of things are done.

"Appropriate" care does *not* mean doing everything that might have some positive payoff, no matter how small or unlikely the payoff or how large the cost. Thus inappropriate care could have some small marginal value to a patient—as at point Y in Figure 5—but a value that does not justify the costs of providing that treatment.

The reasoning behind such a definition is summarized by what economists call "opportunity cost." When resources are spent on activities with low payoffs, we give up the opportunity to use those resources more productively somewhere else. This is clearly true *within* health care. Another "cardiac cath lab" can mean less money is available for childhood immunizations.

It is also true that it would be foolish to try to solve this problem by just increasing what we spend on health care without limit, in order to "do everything." The resources we would use also have an opportunity cost—albeit outside of health care. When we spend more on health, we have less to spend on the environment, crime, education, defense, deficit reduction, or even lowering taxes. The idea is summed up in the only funny idea ever to come from the "dismal science" of economics—and it is not even that funny: TANSTAAFL—an acronym for "There Ain't No Such Thing As A Free Lunch."

Judging appropriateness is difficult—exactly because of the limits on our medical knowledge. Yet insofar as we can evaluate this kind of quality, America has a mixed record. Many observers praise the sophistication and judgment of American physicians. However, the variations in practice patterns noted previously suggest that a nontrivial amount of inappropriate care is being provided by the system. Using the judgment of expert panels as a reference point, some studies suggest that between 25 and 30 percent of many common surgical procedures are inappropriate. Perhaps this is why Americans get more surgery per capita than the citizens of any other industrial nation, yet live no longer.

One explanation of such variations focuses on the effects of capacity on use. This is summarized by an old maxim in health care research called "Roemer's Law"—named for a researcher at UCLA, Milton Roemer. The law is, "A bed built is a bed filled." Obviously the "law" doesn't always hold. Otherwise U.S. hospital occupancy rates would not be only 60 percent! But it can be helpful as a way to understand specific patterns—especially when doctors are making utilization decisions in the presence of significant clinical ambiguity and fee-for-service reimbursement.

Consider for example a procedure I have discussed before, coronary artery bypass graft surgery (or CABG), which is a very profitable operation under current DRG reimbursement. In 1985, a unit to do such surgery was opened at a hospital in Manchester, New Hampshire. Previously most CABGs on Manchester residents had been done in Boston. During the first four years of the Manchester program, the rate of CABGs performed on Manchester residents more than doubled! And there are many, many examples of the same phenomenon at work all around the nation.

There are other indications that the country may be spending too much on low-productivity uses. In international studies of medical decision making, U.S. doctors confronted with the same hypothetical cases advocated noticeably more aggressive treatment than their German or Canadian counterparts. Some international differences in utilization are especially striking. Researchers made a careful comparison of practice patterns among general internists in the United States and United Kingdom for patients with uncomplicated hypertension. They found that U.S. doctors ordered forty times more electrocardiograms, seven times more chest X-rays, and five times more blood tests than did their United Kingdom counterparts. Indeed overall, Americans get roughly four times as many X-rays per capita as their counterparts in the United Kingdom.

To be fair, the United States is not the only country where the inappropriate overuse of certain kinds of medical care is a problem. Both Germany and Japan use drugs and pharmaceuticals at a noticeably higher rate than we do. And there is substantial evidence that, in Japan, these rates are excessive to the point of adversely affecting the population's health. The Japanese example is especially interesting because it reveals the pervasive and cross-cultural effect of economic incentives. Japan's physicians retain practice patterns derived from Chinese herbal medicine— many have traditionally been their own pharmacists. No wonder they prescribe so much.

Appropriateness is not the only dimension of quality. Once decisions are made, they must be implemented. The operation must be performed, the X-ray interpreted, etc. This dimension of quality is perhaps best called "skill." How well do providers do when they actually implement the process of diagnosis and treatment?

Here we have almost no "hard" evidence. Many experienced observers do rate our practitioners very highly. Not only doctors, but nurses, technicians, therapists, and other "allied health workers" are often trained to very high standards in the United States. The extent to which international patients travel to the United States for care suggests that many around the world share this view.

On the other hand, there is one aspect of "skill" that is worrisome in the United States—and that arises from the competitively driven overcapacity in our system. Consider the following comparison. In 1987, on a per capita basis, there were three times as many hospitals providing open heart surgery in California as in Ontario, and five times as many MRI machines. And half the California open heart surgery programs performed fewer than 200 procedures per year. In general, Canada, Germany, and Japan all concentrate their most expensive and advanced medical technology in teaching hospitals to a much greater extent than the United States does.

The skill problem created by our division of effort lies in the old maxim "practice makes perfect." Teams that do fewer procedures per year just cannot be as experienced and skillful as those that operate more frequently. In addition, poor skill increases costs because someone has to pay for the resulting complications and rehospitalizations. For this reason, the Medicare program in recent years has sought to restrict the sites at which certain procedures can be performed to selected high-volume locations.

The third aspect of quality has to do with the interpersonal and humane aspects of the system. That is, how good is the "caring" that we offer? This has several dimensions: Do we offer patients appropriate emotional support? Do we respect their views and preferences? Do we effectively undertake basic physical care tasks like pain control? Do we deal well with family members?

Here again the American record is mixed. While some studies are underway, sound international comparisons are not yet possible. Two points are clear, however. First, smaller community hospitals tend to do better on these dimensions (as reported in surveys of patients themselves) compared to large academic medical centers. Given the complexity of the latter's organizational structures, and their conflicting missions, that may not be too surprising. In addition, when such teaching centers are also public hospitals, they do less well still. Thus, there does remain in America a strong holdover of the system of "two-class medicine" that some hoped would be eliminated by Medicare and Medicaid. To fully explain this point we need to go back and fill in some additional history.

Before 1965, poor people were typically taken care of as "charity" patients—and treated mainly by doctors in training (that is by residents and interns). Thus, they were often treated in public hospitals. In other teaching hospitals, they were housed in separate wards—or even in separate buildings—away from the paying patients. One goal of Medicare and Medicaid was to end this system.

Medicare and Medicaid have in fact done a lot to change the

medical landscape in this regard. Yet thanks to the tight budgets and the often difficult conditions faced by public teaching hospitals, the data suggest that we have a way to go in regard to equity on the "care" dimension of quality. (There are also serious problems with regard to equity of access, which we discuss shortly.)

The second point about "caring" quality is that it varies significantly from hospital to hospital. The range of variation among hospitals of a given type is greater than the variation between types of hospitals. From the viewpoint of hospital managers, this is actually good news. It suggests that management matters—that how a hospital is run does make a difference in its performance. From a systems perspective, however, such variation suggests that there is substantial room for improvement in "care" in many institutions.

The final dimension of quality, namely "amenity," is the one consumers have the least trouble judging. Administrators and trustees have felt free to spend money here—exactly because this seems like a way to attract business. Thus, some hospitals compete fiercely on such "hotel" outputs as meals, parking, air conditioning, and the newness of their facilities. This has gone so far that many maternity services now have wine lists and offer "candlelight" dinners for new parents after birth. But the biggest impact has been on physical plant. And as a result, the United States has the newest and fanciest hospital buildings in this corner of the solar system.

Consider the following example. Some years ago a medical school and teaching hospital, in the mid-Atlantic region, decided to build a new building. Plans were drawn by an eminent hospital architect—known for his "advanced" thinking. The bids from potential construction companies were all far over the available budget. The hospital then hired the architectural unit of a for-profit hospital chain to develop cost-reducing design changes. One set of suggestions, which would have saved several million dollars, concerned simplifying the outer facade of the building. This was rejected out-of-hand. As one trustee put it, "This is a world-famous teaching hospital and it is going to look like a world-famous teaching hospital."

In sum, our national quality record is mixed. We do great on amenities and reasonably well on skill. Care among socio-economic groups is uneven. And on appropriateness there are reasons to be concerned.

Part of the answer to our central paradox then may lie in these quality failures. We may well spend too much on some things that are not tightly linked to improved medical outcomes, like amenities, facilities, and inappropriate care. Such practices would lead us to spend more and get less than nations that do not succumb to such patterns.

Who Gets What

Another major determinant of the effect of care on outcomes is access—namely how, when, and how much care is utilized by different population groups.

From the viewpoint of total utilization, Americans often get less total care—inpatient or outpatient—than other countries, despite our very high expenditures. We have among the lowest overall rates of physician visits and hospital admissions per capita. For example, in Germany citizens enjoy approximately 12 doctor visits per year versus 5.5 per year here. Even the least expensive European systems, the United Kingdom and Denmark, whose costs are less than 40 percent of ours, enjoy a slightly greater number of physician visits per capita than does the United States.

Apart from overall utilization, access is in many ways a comparative question. It varies across income, geographic, and racial lines—even within systems that provide "universal" insurance. Equal nominal eligibility does not automatically result in equal utilization—given social, cultural, economic, and transportation barriers. Moreover, when it comes to influencing health status, it is not absolute levels of utilization that matter, but those levels in relation to underlying rates of disease.

There is no question that in America the access enjoyed by different populations is quite unequal. The low-income, uninsured population receives far less outpatient care than their insured counterparts. But their inpatient hospital admission rates are similar to those of the privately insured. The Medicaid population has relatively high outpatient utilization (partly due to very high rates of ER utilization) *and* high inpatient utilization. Both the uninsured and Medicaid patients stay longer in the hospital, once they are admitted, than the privately insured.

Data on utilization by income level are difficult to come by from other industrial countries. But some useful comparative information is available from Australia. Australia has a high ratio of physicians to population. Its health insurance scheme covers essentially everyone without private insurance. And it pays doctors the same fees for caring for everyone. Under such circumstances lower-income Australians actually use *more* care, both inpatient and outpatient, than their upper-income counterparts, more or less like the Medicaid population in the United States. This is apparently because there, as here, lower-income individuals tend to be sicker. So the higher outpatient use by lower-income levels—not the lower use by the low-income uninsured in the United States—is actually what one would expect when there are not high barriers to access.

The overall high utilization of hospital care by lower-income individuals conceals some important, if contradictory, trends. The high utilization by the poor occurs, in part, because they are far more likely to be hospitalized for two kinds of conditions. First are so-called "ambulatory care sensitive conditions." These are conditions like asthma or the complications of diabetes for which one might expect to avoid—or at least minimize—hospitalization through good ambulatory care. Second there are what can be called "behaviorally sensitive conditions"—like the complications of drug and alcohol use and the effects of violence. Admission rates for these too are elevated in poor areas.

This relationship is powerfully illustrated by data in New York State that describe income and admission rates by zip code, for those under age sixty-five. In the areas with the highest percentage of households in the lowest income bracket, individuals were four times as likely to be hospitalized for ambulatory care sensitive conditions as those from the highest-income zip codes. In the over-sixty-five age group, Medicare coverage seemed to eliminate the income effect.

On the other hand, admission rates for what might be termed "discretionary" procedures are noticeably lower in poor communities compared to more affluent neighborhoods. Such procedures include cardiac surgery and hip replacements. Specific studies of selected high-tech procedures have shown that individuals who are poor or members of minority groups tend to receive such procedures noticeably less frequently.

Lower-income and minority individuals do face a variety of barriers, even beyond financial obstacles, when it comes to utilizing care. These range from having to deal with a different language and culture, to transportation hassles, to lost income from time away from work. At many points during the process, doctors and patients can experience the sorts of breakdowns in their relationship that deflect patients from having surgery: missed appointments, miscommunication across class and cultural boundaries, lack of mutual trust, and so on. Then there is also the fact that poor patients do generate less money for providers—because Medicaid pays less than other insurers and the uninsured often don't pay very much at all.

Moreover, many physicians are reluctant to practice among the poor and the geographically isolated. Studies of large metropolitan areas have shown that the proportion of physicians to population varies widely between more affluent areas and low-income, minority neighborhoods. Thus, we must realize that not all access difficulties experienced by underserved populations would be immediately remedied by a system of universal insurance coverage.

There is a link between these access patterns and the high-cost/modest outcome paradox. The failure to provide better access to ambulatory care for the poor increases their use of expensive hospital care. On the other hand, the lower use by the poor of discretionary procedures may be cost decreasing in the short run—at the price of diminishing the quality and quantity of their lives. Thus, universal coverage will have offsetting effects. Better ambulatory care for the currently underserved could lower hospital costs. More equitable access to certain discretionary procedures could raise hospital costs. It is not clear what the relative magnitude of the two effects will be.

The High Costs of Keeping Up with the Joneses

Another explanation of the high-cost/modest outcome paradox appears to lie in the ways in which health care is organized in the United States versus other countries. The resulting differences in the number of hospitals that offer high-tech services, how frequently those services are utilized, and their administrative costs are quite significant.

We noted earlier the multiplication of high-tech equipment and services in American hospitals, and the possible quality effects of each hospital not doing enough—even as it also encourages inappropriately high rates of surgery for the system as a whole. But the cost effects of such fragmentation can also be substantial. In the United States we spend money on additional, expensive, excess capacity when the patients treated at such sites could have been cared for elsewhere at low incremental cost. Meanwhile, the excess capacity itself is not fully used, and the equipment, dedicated space, and specially trained personnel cannot be shifted to other activities.

There is some evidence from detailed studies comparing Canada and the United States that the United States pays a price in just this way for its multiple competitive providers. For example, in 1987 the costs per occupied hospital bed were $38,000 in Germany, $50,000 in the Netherlands, and $182,000 in the United States. Canada, with more admissions and longer lengths of stay, has hospital costs 15 to 25 percent below the United States—even *after* adjusting for differences in case mix and wage rates. And at least some of that apparently can be attributed to less efficient use of people and machines in the United States.

Ironically, some of our recent effort to save costs by shortening lengths of stay could be contributing to this problem. We are trying to do so much so fast in American hospitals these days that it may be costing us extra to get the job done. In short stays, there is less flexibility for scheduling patients for tests and treatments, since they have to go home so soon. Hence more capacity is required, and the resulting peaks and valleys in demand produce less efficient capacity utilization.

Competitive fragmentation also increases administrative costs. Each insurance company, and each government program, has its own forms and its own rules. There are all those bills to be sent out and all those different payments to keep track of, not to mention all the fights to be had with insurance companies over specific cases.

A competitive system also confronts hospitals with a score of larger issues. They have to try to negotiate deals with HMOs, create managed-care networks, and keep track of all their various subsidiaries. Then there are all the worries over strategic planning, marketing, financial management, and public relations. In many other national systems little, if any, of this goes on. As a result, administration is the fastest-growing component of American hospital budgets. United States hospitals spend more than twice as much as their Canadian counterparts on billing and administration. And the number of health care administrators in the United States is rising four times faster than the number of doctors.

Detailed international comparisons on this point can be quite startling. I have studied one typical German hospital in a manufacturing region in southern Germany. At a bit over 700 beds, it is one of the more sophisticated hospitals in the region—just a step below the nearby university teaching hospital. The hospital has a sparkling glass and chrome lobby filled with plants, surgical and medical intensive-care units, and a helipad directly outside of the emergency room entrance. The helipad is used for trauma and for transporting patients to the nearby teaching hospital— which performs organ transplants and other highly specialized services. From a clinical perspective, this hospital looks very similar to a large community hospital in the suburbs of a major city in the United States.

Since many hospital employees work part-time, staffing is best understood by asking how many full-time employees it would require to perform the work. Looking at this number (called Full-Time Equivalents or FTEs), we find that this hospital has only sixty FTEs of administrative employees! For anyone who has spent any time in a 700-bed hospital in the United States, this is a staggering fact. The typical American community hospital of this size would literally have *at least* ten times as many administrators—in the vicinity of 700! In the United States such institutions tend to have the equivalent of one full-time administrative employee per bed.

How does this German hospital do it? Twenty-five FTEs are responsible for billing, admissions, and phones, three take care of bookkeeping and accounting, eight handle personnel, two are cashiers, one collects bad debt, five are payroll clerks, four do medical records, two are information resources experts, two are secretaries for the administration, two are security guards, and three purchase supplies. Finally, there is a top management team of *three*. There are comparably sized American hospitals that have more administrative personnel in their emergency departments alone!

Most international comparisons of administrative costs do not include these costs inside the delivery system. Instead they tend to focus on the insurance sector. Here, too, the United States spends a disproportionate amount. The cost of public and private insurance overhead and profits is 5.9 percent of personal health care expenditures in the United States and 1.4 percent in Canada. And that is 1.4 percent of a number that is much lower.

It is also the case that the *total* number of hospital personnel in the United States is *two or even three times as high* as in other countries. Here it is important to compare personnel per occupied bed—not personnel per bed—since the United States has so much lower occupancy levels than most other nations. In most of the world, that number is two to three FTEs per occupied bed. In the United States it is five to six FTEs. And our numbers are relatively low since these data leave out the employees of firms that do work for hospitals on contract—a practice much more prevalent in the United States.

There are, of course, many complexities to any such comparison. The United States does have shorter lengths of stay, and we do more surgery on an outpatient basis (now 50 percent of all surgery in the United States, adjusted for complexity). Also we have fewer admissions because less severely ill medical cases are now not admitted at all. As a consequence, the typical patients in U.S. hospitals are sicker than their counterparts in other countries.

If the American pattern of fewer admissions and shorter lengths of stay really is sensible, we should be *saving* money by behaving in this way. That is, the cost savings from fewer admissions and shorter lengths of stays should be more than the extra costs we incur by treating patients more intensively while they are hospitalized. So while severity differences may explain some differences across countries in *average* daily costs, they cannot explain why our whole hospital system costs so much more, despite the fact that it produces fewer hospital days per capita.

It does seem that competitively generated duplication of facilities and service, not to mention the luxurious physical plants we have built, play a role in our higher costs. So too do our very high staffing levels. For these all lead to the inefficient use of buildings, people, and equipment. The explosion in administrative costs in response to rising hospital entrepreneurship, and growing insurance company intrusiveness, also seems quite important. We have created substantial managerial empires in many of our larger hospitals—next to which our German comparison institution looks implausibly austere. As the old saying goes, "You pays your money and you takes your choice." It is not clear that within the system competitive fragmentation has led us to choose very wisely.

Fix It Before It Breaks

A precept of the Total Quality Management approach to production is that the worst way to deal with a quality problem is after it has occurred. "Defect finding" forces the "customer" of a "product" to suffer two costs: the cost of poor product performance and the cost of "repair and rework" to improve that performance. The alternative, the quality gurus argue, is to keep defects from appearing in the first place.

As a metaphor for the health care system, this analysis suggests that another explanation for our high costs is a lack of attention to the problems of prevention. Rather than "repair and rework"—i.e., medical care once folks are sick—what more could we do to prevent disease in the first place?

The U.S. emphasis on spending for the sick can be seen in various ways. Britain, with much lower per capita spending, focuses a much greater share of its available resources on community-based services. Perhaps as a result, British health expenditures per child are more than twice the spending on each prime-age adult, whereas the United States spends only one-third as much on each child as on each adult.

The quality-control metaphor does have its limits. While much prevention does save money, not all does. A successful outreach program that helps pregnant teens improve their eating habits, and encourages them to give up tobacco, alcohol, and drugs while pregnant, probably is cost saving. Such behavioral changes are likely to raise the birth weights of their babies, and the resulting lifetime savings in medical and social cost could be very significant.

On the other hand, it is possible for prevention to increase health care costs—if it substitutes expensive lives and deaths for what would have been relatively inexpensive demises. At least one British government study argued that ending cigarette smoking would greatly increase the costs of the National Health Service—not to mention those of the pension funds—since non-smokers would live longer and on balance use more resources. The point is that lung cancer often kills people exactly at the point in their lives where they would start incurring high costs for other ailments.

Some have even argued that motorcycle helmets have the same effect, keeping alive expensive-to-care-for accident victims who otherwise would have died much more cheaply. On the other hand, if helmets do reduce injury severity, they will tend to lower health care costs. And the data for both cigarettes and helmets are ambiguous. Still these possibilities make the point that prevention—like health care itself—can be valuable for the *gains* it produces, even if on balance it costs, rather than saves, money.

Given the role of behavior in causing current patterns of disease, it is not obvious that doctors are the group best equipped to play the lead role in prevention efforts. Do physicians really know all that much about preventing substance abuse or street violence? Instead a whole series of indirect efforts, from economic development and job training to better housing and gun control, may be where some of the most effective leverage points are to be found. And a whole series of techniques, from media campaigns, to school-based programs, to neighborhood organizing, are likely to be a part of any well-designed effort.

Insofar as the medical world connects at all to these problems, it is likely to be through multidisciplinary groups working within the traditionally underfunded arena of public health. Thus, one of the critical questions to ask about any health care reform effort is what will be its impact on such programs.

Money is likely to be so "tight" that the government will engage in various sleight-of-hand efforts to find the necessary funds. As a result, specialized public health programs could be discontinued on the grounds that they were unnecessary in the new universal system. Meanwhile, well-entrenched entities, like the teaching hospitals, will jealously guard their share of the pie (e.g., by protecting the indirect teaching-cost adjustment under Medicare), even as low-budget, community-based agencies risk getting frozen out.

The same concerns are also relevant when it comes to prevention efforts within the more conventional health care system. Such efforts are often labeled "primary" or "secondary," depending on whether they are devoted to detecting disease or altering behavior once disease has been discovered. Pap smears or mammograms to detect cervical or breast cancer are primary prevention. Getting a middle-aged man who has had a heart attack to stop smoking is secondary prevention. The risk we run in any health care reform effort is that pressures to save costs in the short run could actually decrease the attention the system devotes to such efforts—even where they are cost effective.

Where Does the Money Come From

A final feature of our review of the performance of the U.S. system takes us away from our central paradox and back to an issue of basic equity. Who pays for this, the most expensive health care system on earth? And how are we to judge the distribution of payments?

Economists often use "proportionality" as a guide to tax equity. A proportional tax increases as income increases. A progressive tax (like the income tax) goes up faster than income. Regressive taxes (like a sales tax) also go up with income—only more slowly than income. Thus the poor pay a higher proportion of their income in taxes than do the well-to-do when we use a regressive tax.

Evaluating the impact of the U.S. health care financing system is as complex as the financing system itself. But one feature stands out. *The bulk of the funds are raised in a way that has little or no relation to ability to pay.* In this too, the United States is alone in the world.

First consider the 60 percent of health care expenditures that do not come from government. These come from insurance premiums or out-of-pocket expenditures by individuals. In either case, an individual's income does not affect what he or she has to pay. Premium-based financing is like a "head tax"—a flat rate per person. This is an extremely regressive tax because it does not vary at all with income. When Margaret Thatcher proposed such a scheme for financing local government costs in Britain, she was deposed by the *Conservative* party as overly mean-spirited. Yet that is the major source of health care financing in the United States today.

Moreover, the favorable tax treatment of health insurance contributions is especially valuable to upper-income individuals at higher tax brackets. In 1991 this tax treatment saved beneficiaries nearly $70 billion in federal taxes yearly—26 percent of which went to the 10 percent of households with incomes over $75,000 and only 6 percent to the more than 30 percent of households with incomes under $20,000.

Tracing out the source of the 40 percent of costs that are publicly financed is even more complicated. Medicare Part A funds come from a payroll tax, and so are raised in a way that is roughly proportional to income—although slightly regressive because of the upper limit on how much income is taxed. Medicaid and Medicare Part B are funded by both state and federal general tax revenues. Deciding who pays these funds means guessing which taxes were raised—or which other expenditures curtailed— to pay for these costs.

Trying to do such an analysis would lead us too far afield, especially in the presence of substantial disagreement among economists about how one should proceed. Suffice it to say that overall our health care financing system is much less progressive than any other nation's. Unlike the United States, they rely on payroll taxes, and in many cases general revenue from progressive taxes, to support their programs. The consequences of our policies are clear. The bottom 10 percent of the country, in terms of income, receives 1.3 percent of income and pays 3.9 percent of health care costs. The top 10 percent receives 33.8 percent of income and pays only 21.7 percent of costs. As a result, per capita spending on health care was 20 percent of family income in the poorest 10 percent of the population and 8 percent in the richest decile.

Lives in the Balance

The implications of this review of the performance of the American health care system are a bit unsettling. We spend more than any other nation, don't live as long as most, and actually get fewer services. Health care costs are increasing so rapidly that they threaten to create ever more serious problems for business and government. We may have very well-trained personnel and sumptuous facilities, but the system is at risk of being buried under an avalanche of paperwork and administrative costs. It is not clear that access to care is either fair or cost effective, that treatment appropriateness is all that it could be, or that we are spending anywhere near enough on prevention—even though that may involve mainly nonmedical interventions. And we finance all this in a way that takes little account of ability to pay. Maybe then the distress we saw in Chapter 1 really is justified. Maybe, slowly brewing just under the surface, there is more of a health care crisis than the newly energized public yet realizes. But if that is the case, what should or can we do?

5

REFORMING THE HEALTH CARE SYSTEM: The Alternatives

No Easy Answers

Consider the performance of the system we have just reviewed, or rather, as many critics put it, the "nonsystem." Some of its flaws are the result of deep underlying forces. Some flow from the behavior of the institutions that make up the nonsystem, both on the insurance and on the provider side. The question is, how do we restructure this nonsystem while still preserving those features which have drawn researchers, students, and patients from around the world?

If we want a new "system," do we just make it up? Do we copy other countries? Taking bits and pieces of different national plans will not necessarily produce a coherent set of arrangements. And the practices of other nations cannot just be transported wholesale into a completely different cultural, economic, and political context. On the other hand, restructuring a particularly vital one seventh of our nation's economy on the basis of a new scheme that, while plausible, has never actually been tried, seems very risky.

The fundamental ethical and practical choices involved in health care reform have not changed over the past twenty years. Do we guarantee universal coverage or just try to expand coverage voluntarily? Do we create a new public system or merely add to our existing patchwork set of arrangements? Which benefits will be covered under the plan? Where will the money come from? And how can we keep costs from spinning even further out of control?

The current interest in reform has not arisen because we suddenly have a new and perfect alternative. Rather the situation has become so unsatisfactory that some of the same old options are now being taken more seriously. As a nation, we seem increasingly prepared to follow another piece of Yogi Berra's advice. "When you come to a fork in the road, take it." If there were a simple, proven answer to the nation's health care woes, health care reform would already have been accomplished.

Reform alternatives range from plans that rely on slightly modified free markets to totally government-run health care. Free market advocates want to use health insurance and health care markets in the same way markets function for any other good, by having consumers decide not to buy from inefficient providers. They focus their efforts on influencing the behavior of consumers and improving their shopping decisions. Their approach, they say, is the only one that respects the American values of free choice and market competition.

Proponents at the other end of the spectrum argue that health care fundamentally shapes citizens' capacities to lead satisfactory lives. As such, it should be viewed as a right, and guaranteed by the government. They argue that there are distributional and technical reasons that make a universal system, with a substantial public role, highly desirable. In particular, individual patients do not determine the demand for many health care services. Physicians, acting as the patients' agents, do. Therefore, these reformers would focus on shaping and constraining the behavior of medical providers, and on limiting the total resources allocated to the health care sector.

The underlying issue concerns the extent to which we should

view health care as a "public good." For economists, a "public good"—unlike a "private good"—is one where individual consumption decision have effects well beyond the person doing the consuming. The contrast is illustrated by the difference between low-lead gasoline and breakfast cereal. Society has little interest in what you or I eat for breakfast (whether it is granola or Frosted Flakes). But the lead content of gasoline influences the pollution our cars generate, and the quality of the air that many, many others have to breathe.

Advocates of market-oriented strategies see health care as primarily a "private good." Like breakfast cereal, decisions about it can be left to individual consumers. Those at the other end of the spectrum stress the "public good" aspects of these same decisions. All of us, they say, will pay for the fiscal and social consequences of poor primary care, unnecessary heart surgery, or duplicate and surplus high-tech imaging capacity. Therefore they want to use accountable, public processes to make the key resource allocation decisions.

Plans at the ends of the political spectrum are not all that relevant to the U.S. context. We are not likely to embrace a pure free market scheme, with special savings accounts or insurance vouchers for the poor. Nor will we employ a British-style, government-operated system. Instead, centrist reform options, particularly "managed competition" or a "single-payer" system with care provided by the existing system of doctors and hospitals, are the most relevant. And we will discuss each of these in turn.

Designing a Five-Legged Beast—Managed Competition

"Managed competition" is a quintessentially American idea. It is also still a largely theoretical construct. As Representative Fortney "Pete" Stark has said, it is a "five-legged beast." It might be possible to design one that works, but there aren't any examples in nature. Similarly Representative Dan Rostenkowski, the powerful chairman of the House Ways and Means Committee, commenting on its complexity, likens it to "the domestic equivalent of star wars." Still, the idea does build on American experience with HMOs and on a lot of contemporary economic theory. The scheme won the attention of Bill Clinton, the "new" Democrat, in part because it seems like something other than old-fashioned, heavy-handed government intervention.

The concept of managed competition has wide political appeal. Conservatives, who prefer private markets and oppose expanding government, have been attracted to the "competition" component. Liberals, who doubt that market mechanisms will provide equitable universal access, like the "managed" aspect. The very ambiguity of the idea has helped it gain political momentum, since pragmatists who just want to pass something have been quick to join the managed-competition bandwagon. Indeed one important Senate health staffer has justified his support in just such terms. "I know it is imperfect," he said, "but it can pass. And we can always go back and fix it later."

The theory was largely constructed by Alain Enthoven, a Stanford University health economist, and his colleagues in the "Jackson Hole Group"—a group of business executives, academics, and health care managers who have been meeting periodically for several years in Jackson Hole, Wyoming. They offer a two-part diagnosis of our current problems.

First, many Americans have too much health insurance. Most insurance plans are too generous because they do not impose enough financial incentives on individuals to use less care, nor do they direct them to efficient providers. Moreover, Americans choose these insurance plans because they do not pay enough attention to the relative cost and cost effectiveness of alternative kinds of coverage. This is because several provisions of the tax code guarantee that government will share some of each employee's health insurance costs. And the more costly the plan, and the higher the employee's income, the larger the subsidy. This in turn lessens the incentives felt by both employers and employees to shop aggressively for health insurance.

Secondly, consumers have been prevented from doing such shopping by many employers, who offer them little or no choice of insurance plans. Even when employees do have choices, their own lack of information, and the difficulties of comparing various nonstandardized alternatives, makes them less responsive to price differences.

To correct all this, the proponents of managed competition would introduce a complex set of reforms that would transform the markets for health insurance and health care. First they would create a National Health Board that would, among other tasks, define a "standard" benefit package. Since price competition would occur among plans offering these standard benefits, customers would be better able to compare prices. Another new national organization, the Outcome Standards Management Board, would define performance and quality measures which all plans would have to publicly report. These could be used by consumers to evaluate their options.

Second, a whole series of nonprofit insurance purchasing entities would be established, to act on behalf of all small employers and individauls in a geographic area. These "Health Insurance Purchasing Cooperatives" (HIPCs) or "Health Alliances" would be skilled, large-scale buyers. They would provide smaller employers and individuals with the same advantages that many large employers currently enjoy—including market power, lower administrative costs, and the ability to pool risks. Large employers would have the option of joining these Health Alliances or acting on their own. The size at which large employers would be allowed to function independently is likely to be a source of great contention, as we will later explain.

Third, each Health Alliance would negotiate with comprehensive-care networks (referred to as Accountable Health Partnerships or Accountable Health Plans, i.e., AHPs) to provide the medical services included in the standard benefit package for a per capita annual fee. These AHPs could be HMOs. Or they could be combinations of insurance companies and provider networks—which would necessarily begin to look a lot like HMOs. Establishing the AHPs would transform the sellers of health care in each area from a large number of fragmented providers into a much smaller number of vertically integrated, comprehensive producers. The AHPs would presumably have every incentive to organize themselves efficiently, in order to keep down costs and eliminate unnecessary tests and treatments.

Individuals would choose among the AHPs that were offered for purchase by their Health Alliances. The resulting price and value competition among the AHPs would mean that those which are inefficient and high cost would soon lose enrollees. Since inefficient plans presumably contain inefficient providers, high-cost doctors and hospitals would face pressure from their AHPs to control their costs—or they would all lose enrollment. This two-step effect—consumers shop for AHPs and AHPs pressure providers—is critical to managed competition's potential for controlling health care costs.

Many details about how the Alliances would function, and their relationships to the AHPs, have yet to be decided. In most schemes all payments would be made to the Alliances, which would in turn pay the plans. This opens up the possibility of using the Alliances to provide various kinds of cross-subsidies to the poor or unemployed, without the now anathema mechanism of higher taxes. In addition, it is not clear if the Alliances would be required to make available all the qualified plans in their area, or if they would be able to make a preliminary shopping decision to narrow the field.

Finally, the tax code would also have to be changed. Today all employer, and some employee, contributions to health insurance costs are not treated as taxable income to employees. The new scheme would treat payment for health insurance above a certain level as part of an individual's taxable income—whether this was paid by employers or employees. The most common proposal is to set the relevant threshold at the cost of the least expensive plan in each region that offers the standard benefit package and that meets federal quality standards. Above that level, everyone would have to pay insurance costs with after-tax dollars. Health insurance payments by the self-employed would receive the same dual treatment. This would amount to more generous tax treatment than the rules for itemized deductions currently allow.

Since many individuals cannot afford or may not choose to purchase insurance, managed competition does not guarantee universal coverage. Some combination of public financing, reform of the insurance markets, or required purchases will be necessary if everyone is to be brought into the system.

One widely discussed option would be to combine a so-called "employer mandate" with an "individual mandate." This would require all employers to offer health insurance to their employees, which those employees would be required to purchase. The self-employed and the otherwise uninsured would also be required to purchase insurance. Premiums would be based on a sliding-scale government subsidy, since some individuals could afford to pay little or nothing toward their own insurance costs. The attraction of an employer mandate is that it appears to finance coverage for the uninsured without raising taxes. In fact, of course, workers and consumers (i.e., everyone) will pay for the mandated coverage through higher prices or lower wages.

An employer mandate could be financed in various ways. The most obvious way would be to have employers pay a portion of the premium for the least costly standard plan in their region (say 75 percent to 80 percent), leaving the individual to pay the rest, and any differential if he or she chooses a higher-cost plan. This, however, could amount to a relatively high percentage of existing compensation in small business and in other businesses with low-wage workers. One way to cross-subsidize such firms would be to limit total employer plus employee payments to some percentage of total wages. The Health Alliance would then have to find funds to make up the difference, either from other employers or through some public subsidy.

Requiring everyone to purchase insurance, and even subsidizing their costs, would still not guarantee that everyone would be able to buy coverage for a reasonable price. Insurance could still be exorbitantly expensive, or even unavailable, for those already sick. Hence, universal coverage under managed competition would also require substantial reform of the insurance market. First, while prices may vary among plans, each plan would have to charge everyone the same price for the standard benefit package—so-called "community rating." Second, no health plan could refuse to cover anyone who applied, nor could it exclude coverage for any preexisting condition when someone moved from one plan to another. Third, to enable those who are dissatisfied to switch plans, all plans would have to have an annual "open enrollment" period, to allow subscribers to change membership. According to the Jackson Hole version of managed competition, ensuring that all this occurred would be the responsibility of yet a third new national organization: the National Insurance Standards Board.

Estimates of the additional costs for universal coverage under managed competition range from $30 billion to over $100 billion, depending on the generosity of the standard benefit package and the extent of the subsidy scheme. Limiting the tax deductibility of employer and employee contributions to the cost of the least costly plan in each region would make excess contributions taxable income for employees. This could generate as much as $20 billion in new tax revenue. "Sin" taxes on tobacco and liquor are also a frequently suggested option, although alone they probably could not provide the necessary revenue. Another possible funding source is a "windfall" tax, which would apply to any providers that generate excessive profits because of increased coverage for, and revenue from, the uninsured and underinsured. Yet another option is to finance the scheme from the cost savings—to either government or private insurers—that might come about from successful cost control. Capturing those savings, and getting them to the Alliances in the form of actual cash, will be no easy task.

Opponents of managed competition are not convinced that this whole structure will accomplish its intended purposes. They offer six major arguments, all of which are passionately countered by supporters of this approach.

Have I Got a Deal for You

First, will individuals have enough data and sophistication to shop effectively among insurance plans? Critics argue that such choices are incredibly complex. Each plan is a bundle of many different services whose quality and convenience will vary, and for which consumers cannot fully predict their demand. How do you know whether to shop for a plan with the best cardiologist or the best pediatrician, the best mental health care or the best surgeon, before you are sick? And once someone establishes relationships with providers, will they really switch plans to save a few dollars a month? And if they don't, where will the competitive pressure to keep costs down come from?

This was brought home to me recently when my twenty-four-year-old daughter, a biology graduate from Stanford, with a master's degree from Cambridge University in England, called me in desperation. She had to choose a health plan. Please, she asked, could she send me the 150-page booklet she had been given by the state of Maryland about her insurance choices so that I could offer her some advice? When the booklet arrived, it took me several hours to even understand her options. Then I realized that it did not even contain the information I needed to help her; for there was no data that allowed me to judge the quality of the care offered by the competing plans.

Critics also point to the experience in the "Medigap" market for insurance policies to supplement Medicare. They argue that fear and irrationality clearly play a large role in those insurance-purchasing decisions. Many seniors purchase plans that are really bad deals in terms of expert actuarial analysis—paying more to avoid out-of-pocket costs than those costs themselves are likely to be.

Choices made before an uncertain event can look much less attractive after the fact. Suppose I find, unexpectedly, that I do need a good cardiologist? When I go to change plans at the next open enrollment period, all my family's other medical contacts may have to be broken. And suppose my Health Alliance suddenly refuses to include my current plan under its available options for next year? Company benefit managers now often face this dilemma and can testify to the difficulty of switching individuals' or families' coverage just to achieve modest cost savings. Yet as Enthoven has stressed, the whole scheme depends on heightened individual price sensitivity when shopping for health insurance.

Establishing relationships with new providers can also involve substantial costs (new histories and physicals, new medical records), as well as adverse health consequences. Continuity of care has long been valued by patients and doctors as health-improving and cost-reducing. And yet that is exactly what will have to be sacrificed if we are to have aggressive, price-sensitive shopping. Ironically, the sick, who are the ones most likely to have strong ties to certain providers, are likely to be among the most reluctant to switch. Yet to limit total spending, they are exactly those whom it is most important to move into more efficient plans.

Proponents of managed competition agree that initially consumers would have to struggle with the crude or nonexistent data that my daughter and I confronted. They argue, however, that this situation would rapidly improve. The new Outcome Standards Management Board would fund the research needed to develop data that would allow consumers to "shop" effectively.

They also point out that individuals already shop for many complex products that they cannot fully evaluate—from automobiles to college educations. Even in medicine, consumer preferences have influenced patterns of care in certain specialties—such as obstetrics. And there are more and more efforts afoot to educate patients—whether it is video disks on the risks and benefits of surgery or magazine surveys to rate the nation's "best hospitals." Consumerism, they say, is already emerging as a powerful force in health care, and managed competition would only encourage such developments.

900 Billion Dollars Is Real Money

The distinguished, now deceased senator from Illinois Everett Dirksen used to say about federal expenditures, "A million here a million there and soon you are talking real money." It is an ironic feature of the current American fiscal landscape that Dirksen is now generally misquoted as having said, "A billion here, a billion there . . ." Yet even by today's inflated standards, the nearly $900 billion spent on health care is indeed "real money."

This explains the concern behind the second criticism opponents level at managed competition, namely that it would not in fact control health care costs. They argue that there is no evidence that removing the tax free status of the last few dollars of health insurance contributions will make individuals' purchasing decisions that much more price sensitive or cause most people to join tightly managed care networks. Given today's relatively low tax rates, the change in marginal prices will not be that great. And even that modest change may prove politically difficult, which would be a major retreat from the theoretical rational for the whole approach.

Both sides agree that evaluating the cost-containment potential of managed competition involves interpreting the experience of existing HMOs. But they disagree over what to make of the fact that those organizations have lower costs, but similar rates of cost increase, compared to other insurance plans.

Managed competition advocates argue that today's HMOs are the cheapest plans currently available and that their rate increases have been influenced by the limited price sensitivity of customers in the current market. Given that customers are not that influenced by price, some HMOs apparently choose to charge just under the prices of competing fee-for-service plans, letting the latter act as "price leaders." But in the managed-competition scheme, the Health Alliances, as large-scale buyers, will be able to play off plans against each other, and thus induce real price competition. (This assumes the Alliances are not forced to passively accept all qualified AHPs.)

Opponents argue back that the reason for much of the HMOs' cost advantage lies in their patient mix. They tend to attract young, mobile, and healthy subscribers, while sicker patients choose old-fashioned, unmanaged plans. Moreover, they point out that Massachusetts and California have the highest enrollment in HMOs in America, and therefore are most like the managed competitive future. And yet they also have the highest per capita health care costs in the nation.

Opponents even argue that the short-run impact of managed competition could be to *increase* costs. Hospitals might decide that competitive survival requires them to duplicate the services of other hospitals, in order to become "full line producers." (The recent multiplication of maternity services at Boston teaching hospitals—even while birthrates are too low to fill existing capacity—is arguably just such a phenomena.) The result could be excess capacity, whose capital costs would have to be paid for even if the services remain unused.

Another relevant example, critics contend, is airline deregulation. Initially various carriers entered each other's profitable routes and load factors fell. However, unlike airlines, hospitals that lose money cannot shift any excess capacity to other routes. After the competitive "shakeout" among airlines, Eastern Airlines planes could be repainted and flown from Phoenix to Portland by another carrier. Excess maternity capacity in Boston cannot be transformed into a Holiday Inn—still less into a Holiday Inn in Tampa!

Advocates respond that hospitals that make foolish investment decisions will finally be forced to face the consequences of their actions under managed competition. As a result, over time they will be forced to become more effective and judicious competitors. And, in any case, the inefficiency of competition, they suggest, would be less than the inefficiency of a politically controlled system.

No Room at the Inn

A third issue involves the problem of risk adjustment. Given community rating and open enrollment, there will be huge financial incentives for plans to avoid having sick subscribers, especially since the top 10 percent of the population in terms of spending consume 70 percent of health care resources. One way to counteract such incentives would be to have those plans with fewer sick enrollees cross-subsidize plans with higher cost members. The problem is that many opponents (and even some proponents) of managed competition believe that there currently is no adequate method for determining how much to compensate plans whose subscribers are disproportionately poor risks. Easily gathered objective characteristics, like age and sex, explain only a tiny fraction of the cost variation among individuals.

This inability to risk-adjust, critics contend, will also create serious problems for providers who cater to high-cost users. Will they even find plans that will accept them as part of their network? Which network will want to include a neighborhood health center with many multiproblem clients (including AIDS patients) as part of a system financed by community-rated premiums? As one skeptic put it, "What if you threw a [managed competition] party in Harlem and nobody came?"

Ironically, customers will be particularly drawn to low-cost plans that achieve their savings by excluding high-cost subscribers. Such plans will be able to offer much better service, for the same price, than those plans whose low prices are due to ruthless utilization controls. Thus managed competition might actually exacerbate the access problems of the poor and the sick.

Enthoven agrees that "the jury is still out on risk adjusted payment mechanisms." However, with proper regulatory authority and good enough data, he believes the Health Alliances will be able to detect any insurance plan that is risk selecting and take the necessary actions. One way, he suggests, would be to get competing plans to police each other—since the overall risk pool represents a "constant sum" game, in which one plan's gain is another's loss.

It is widely agreed that the experience of the Federal Employees' Health Benefits Program (FEHBP) shows the instability that can result from not effectively "managing" competition. FEHBP covers about 9 million people and resembles what a Health Alliance might look like. Many plans compete for enrollees on an annual basis, with employees paying for the added cost of more expensive plans. Because the FEHBP does not compensate different plans for biased risk selection, prices and enrollment in individual plans have often shifted noticeably year to year. In the past, plans gained and lost market share not because they were more or less efficient, but because they attracted more or less costly individuals. During one two-year period, one third of all subscribers changed plans and premium increases averaged 62 percent, as even the HMOs followed the rate increases of the plans whose subscribers were sicker.

Some of the practices that networks might use to discourage high-cost members will be nearly impossible to regulate. Marketing techniques and benefit packages might be controlled. But some of the measures discussed in Chapter 2 that involve waiting times, or the quality of provider interactions, will be difficult to monitor.

It is clear that risk selection by HMOs is possible, that they can attract and retain healthier individuals. This was revealed by the experience in the 1980s of a federal demonstration project that allowed more than 300,000 Medicare recipients to enroll in twenty-six HMOs. Researchers compared the amount the government paid for three different groups of individuals in the years before the experiment: those who chose to enroll in HMOs and stayed enrolled, those who didn't enroll, and those who enrolled and then disenrolled. The prior health care costs of continuing enrollees were 21 percent below those of nonenrollees. So HMOs got the less expensive people to join their plans. Even more provocatively, disenrollees' preenrollment costs were 50 percent higher than continuing enrollees. So of the people who initially enrolled, the ones who left the HMOs were the most expensive.

Not all HMOs were equally good at such practices. At least one had significant financial troubles, and dropped out of the experiment because it enrolled a disproportionate share of high-cost enrollees. The experiment suggests, however, that most HMOs did a reasonably effective job of attracting and holding on to the least expensive—that is, healthier—individuals. Since HMOs were paid the prior average regional costs of Medicare recipients, the government ended up paying more for HMO coverage for those individuals who stayed with the experiment than they would have paid if they had remained in the ordinary fee-for-service system!

All of this experience raises the specter that managed competition in health care could confront what occurred in the airline industry before deregulation, when competition was "managed" by the now defunct Civil Aeronautics Board. Again and again, new regulations were required to deal with the distortions that previous regulations had created. Eventually even the details of the meals served on airlines were being determined by industry regulators. Ironically, one suggestion for dealing with providers with high-risk clients is to *assign* them to the various networks—just as airlines were once forced to fly unfavorable routes in return for permission to fly more lucrative ones.

How Competitive Will Managed Competition Actually Be?

The next issue concerns the market dynamics of a managed-competition system. Critics contend that these have not been completely thought through. What will happen to hospitals and doctors who are not part of any AHP? Suppose Health Alliances are allowed to shop for and select among AHPs. Then what will happen to entire plans—and their affiliated providers—that do not win the contracts from any, or most, of the Health Alliances in a region in a given year? Surely regulators will be pushed to step in and require that other plans absorb the providers that would otherwise be left out. But then, if all providers need to be in a plan to survive, and all plans have to have contracts with a Health Alliance, how will there be any new entry into these markets?

The threat of competitive entry is critical to the economic

analysis of why competitive markets remain efficient. Otherwise, consider what occurs when there are only a relatively small number of sellers (i.e., an "oligopoly") in a market. Those sellers may soon tire of beating each other's brains out and learn to live together. Such "tacit collusion" or "interdependence recognized" is what economics teaches us to expect in such circumstances. The "oligopoly" starts to behave more and more like a "monopoly" and raises prices. Such a lack of competition could be especially worrisome if due to risk selection, one plan did wind up with a disproportionate share of sicker patients. Then that plan's high rates might serve as a price "umbrella" under which the other plans could peacefully function, with only marginally lower prices.

Some argue that such diminished rivalry is exactly what has happened recently in Minneapolis—long hailed as the example of a competitive HMO-dominated market. These observers suggest that the various HMOs have learned to recognize each other's territory, and have stopped competing vigorously to expand their own market shares.

Many large cities have only two or three teaching hospitals. Why would these hospitals contract with competing plans when they could form their own plan and jointly control all tertiary care? Alternatively, if each is at the core of its own scheme, wouldn't each one eventually learn to cooperate as the plans did in Minneapolis. The Harvard teaching hospitals, for example, recently announced a collaborative effort to "coordinate" their operations. So much for the fierce competition that used to prevail among these institutions!

Again, proponents counter that managed competition already "almost" exists—as in FEHBP—but that it really has not been given the opportunity to blossom because the legal changes required to make it work are not fully in place. An example of what might be achieved, they say, is the success of the California Public Employees Retirement System (CalPERS). CalPERS negotiates health insurance for more than 870,000 individuals who are employees of, or retirees from, most state and public agencies in California (as well as their dependents). It has been able to keep premium increases down in the last few years by using its purchasing power to negotiate big discounts with providers.

Opponents counter that the success that CalPERS has had is really not an indicator that managed competition could contain costs system-wide. When CalPERS limits its premium increases, but overall health care costs increase, it is just using its market power to get providers to shift costs to other payers. In a managed-competition system, there would be no "other payers" to shift costs to.

Finally, opponents argue that there is a limited role for competition in rural areas. Many areas of the country have only one hospital and only one of many types of specialists. Sixty-four of the eighty-three acute care general hospitals in Maine, Vermont, and New Hampshire are the sole hospitals in their local areas. Some estimates suggest that about one third of the nation lives in areas too sparsely populated to support a system based on managed competition. While some proponents of managed competition accept that its scope might be limited in this way, others are not so modest. Health Alliances, they claim, could be quite activist, inducing entry and ensuring effective economic pressure even where it might seem difficult to do so.

How Many Administrators Can Stand on the Head of the "Managed Competition" Pin?

Finally, critics contend that under managed competition the surprisingly high administrative costs that are characteristic of the American system would increase even further. All the new entities, Health Alliances, Accountable Health Plans, and new national regulatory bodies, would have to be created, and staffed and housed as they undertake many new functions. They will have to organize new provider networks, develop methodologies for risk-adjusting payments to the AHPs, take corrective actions against AHPs who appear to be discriminating against high users of care, monitor quality of care, and provide relevant information to subscribers based on types of data that have yet to be developed. All this sounds like a full-employment program for actuaries, health economists, and graduate students interested in health care.

Proponents of managed competition argue that they will reduce administrative costs by standardizing and simplifying all relevant insurance company billing practices and claim forms. They also point out that there are administrative practices that reduce overall system expenditures by eliminating more in the way of unnecessary care than the practices themselves cost. Only those administrative practices will be adopted by "efficient" networks. Any cost-increasing administrative functions would have to make enough of a positive contribution to quality of care that consumers would be willing to pay extra for that care. Opponents remain skeptical that such market-based fine-tuning of product characteristics will actually take place.

Out of Many, One—The "Single-Payer" Option

The appeal of the other major reform alternative—a single-payer scheme modeled on the Canadian system—can be seen by summarizing the arguments against managed competition made by single-payer advocates. The latter simply do not believe that the "shopping" approach will work to control costs. Buyers will not be able to choose effectively, there will not be enough AHPs in most markets, and, even when there are, they will not be rivalrous enough. Also, access for the poor and the sick could deteriorate as plans compete to exclude them. And administrative costs could skyrocket, fueled by the demands of all the new entities.

Instead of all this, single-payer advocates want to sweep away much of the insurance industry—just bulldoze over that part of the swamp—in order to maintain undisturbed much of the current pattern of doctor-patient interaction.

Everyone would be covered by a plan that, since it was universal, would be totally "portable." There would be no need to change insurance coverage when one changed or lost employment. Nor would there be any worries about exclusions for preexisting conditions. Since everyone would be in one risk pool for their entire lifetime, the young would subsidize the elderly and the healthy would subsidize the sick. The system would be financed by payroll taxes or by general revenues, not by premiums, and, therefore, its financing would be based on ability to pay. Of course, individuals would gain back most or all of what they paid in higher taxes through no longer having to spend their own money on health insurance, and possibly through higher wages made possible by an end to employer insurance costs.

All providers would be included and individuals would have free choice of all doctors and hospitals. Physicians and hospitals would be paid on a fee-for-service basis. Hence individual physician incomes and the growth of specific hospitals would depend on customer demand and providers would have every incentive to offer attractive services. Thus they would be more responsive to patients than the salaried employees of HMOs, which could still be integrated into the system. But they would compete for members on the basis of superior quality, not better prices. Overall expenditures would be limited by a global expenditure cap. The proliferation and duplication of expensive technology would be restrained by a planning process linked to the financing of such expenditures.

Proponents argue that such a system would provide equitably financed, seamless coverage for everyone, with a higher share of dollars spent on care, and not administration. Cost shifting and many of the perverse incentives that characterize market-oriented systems, and which actually increase system costs, would be eliminated. Financing based on some measure of ability-to-pay would enable the system to capture revenues from many of those who currently cannot afford insurance premiums but are in fact able and willing to pay something for their health care. Physicians would face less paperwork and much less intrustion into their clinical decision making. Business would be free of many current administrative and financial burdens.

As opposed to managed competition, which is based on empowering the consumers of health care and strengthening the demand side of the market, a single-payer system would control health care costs by limiting the supply of dollars allocated to the system. Single-payer advocates, like doctors Steffie Woolhandler and David Himmelstein at Harvard Medical School, contend that by limiting overall resources, we can turn providers into custodians of the system as a whole. Unless they are faced with a finite supply of resources, the combination of fee-for-service reimbursement, insured patients, and clinical ambiguity will push both doctors and patients to utilize all possible treatments. But once providers know that there are only so many intensive-care beds, or so much liver transplant capacity, they will be forced to accept responsibility for ensuring that it is used where it provides the most benefit to patients. Single-payer advocates believe that influencing physician decision making will do more to contain health care costs than altering consumer behavior.

Advocates of this approach, like political scientist Theodore Marmor at Yale, argue that priority-setting decisions are inevitably part of any health care system. But they say such decisions are now private and implicit. In contrast, in a single-payer scheme explicit trade-offs would have to be faced when the global budget was allocated, just as they are now when Congress fights over the relative worth of the space station or agricultural subsidies when it debates the regular budget. Single-payer advocates believe that only this kind of open, public decision making allows citizens to hold the political process responsible for what is done.

What single-payer advocates apparently envision is the health care analogy to a discussion I witnessed some years ago at a local school board meeting. Insufficient funds meant programs had to be cut. Two alternatives under discussion were junior high school, junior varsity sports and a computer programming course for gifted elementary school students. Each had their advocates. One mother said her athletically and academically not-very-gifted son was nonetheless kept interested in junior high school by junior varsity sports. Another reviewed how much her talented third-grade daughter had learned about computers. Each suggested that the other child's experience represented only a small gain to society. In the end there was no question that both programs did some good. The issue was how to balance the values of competing worthy services when not all worthy services were fundable?

Managed competition advocates argue that, on the contrary, consumer choice is the best way to limit "flat-of-the-curve" spending; that is, spending on treatment that doesn't really help patients. They claim that price-sensitive consumers will not choose to spend their money on insurance plans that offer expensive coverage of low-yield care. Instead, individuals will buy cheaper insurance that, for instance, covers them only for the shrimp cocktail, not the caviar.

The single-payer approach has been plagued by accusations that it would produce long queues for treatment and by labels like "rationing" and "socialized medicine." There are also many who argue that the tax increases that would be required make such a proposal politically impossible—even if citizens would also gain from not having to pay private insurance costs. However, other features of the scheme are sufficiently attractive that the leading single-payer bill has eighty-five co-sponsors—one of the largest health care reform blocks in Congress, and one that includes some of that body's most knowledgeable and influential health care experts.

Single-payer advocates admit that any system which relies on capacity limits to constrain costs will produce waiting lines, like those in Canada today. They argue that every national health insurance scheme has to find some way to control use, in order to control costs. The issue, they say, is not *whether* we ration care, but *how* we ration care. And rationing by a combination of need and first come, first served, they argue, is the fair way to proceed. The United States today, in contrast, relies heavily on price to "ration" care. That means that the poor, and the uninsured, get less—especially, as we saw in Chapter 4, for outpatient services, and certain high-tech care.

Advocates of a single-payer plan point out that in a true market, utilization depends on income. The upper middle class have big boats, the lower middle class have small boats, and the poor swim! Many were offended some years ago when certain wealthy foreigners—who paid more than anyone else—apparently received preferential treatment when it came to "jumping the queue" for organ transplantation in certain hospitals. But on true market principles, there would be nothing wrong with even auctioning off such places to the highest bidder! Most health care reformers on the competitive end of the spectrum wouldn't go that far. But some are quite explicit in saying they want to preserve superior access for the well-to-do—not just with regard to amenities but also with regard to skill and expertise. This is one of the clearest value differences between market-oriented and single-payer advocates.

Setting Explicit Limits

How would global budget limits and reimbursement systems actually work under a single payer plan? First an overall target would be chosen—most likely at a level which ensures that health care spending does not increase faster than the rate of growth of the overall economy. Health care dollars would then be allocated from this fixed pie to various sectors: physicians, hospitals, pharmaceuticals, etc. Initially expenditures would be divided more or less as they are under our current system, although that could change over time in response to changing public priorities. Including all services—inpatient and outpatient—and all providers under such a budget would prevent costs from ballooning out of control in sectors not subject to revenue limits.

Under a single-payer system, physician fees, which currently account for about 20 percent of health care spending, would be determined by a government rate-setting body based on some sort of relative value scale. That method would be similar to the Medicare RBRVS system described in Chapter 3. Regional budget targets would be set (perhaps by states) reflecting both fee levels and expected volumes of care. The insurance fund would withhold a portion of all doctors' fees (say 10 percent) until the end of a pay period, as it does in Germany and in some Canadian provinces. Overall volume would then be tallied and physicians would either receive the full amount withheld or, if volume was above projections, only a portion of it. The adjustment would be made in order to meet the overall budget target.

The intent of such "volume performance" standards would be to give physicians an incentive to accept responsibility as a group for patterns of care. As each physician generates more volume, his or her personal income does increase. But as all physicians generate more volume, the payment that each physician receives per unit of service declines. Thus physicians would be encouraged to develop cooperative arrangements to use the data generated by the payment system for "profile monitoring." This would reveal those whose volume was inconsistent with their patient base. These providers could then be subject to a variety of interventions, from peer pressure, to refresher education, to formal discipline.

Opponents counter that the German system is not relevant to the United States because of structural differences. State medical societies in America are much weaker than their German counterparts and have much less physician loyalty. Thus a sense of group responsibility will be much more difficult to develop in the United States. In Germany, physician organizations *negotiate* the overall budget with the government and then the fee schedule within each specialty group. These negotiations, and the division of physicians into regional and specialty groups, are crucial to the success of the German system. The United States, critics point out, does not have any similar professional negotiating bodies in place, nor are we typically willing to allow such public-private bargaining to determine the use of public money.

Under most versions of a global budget scheme, hospital expenditures would be separated into capital and operating expenditures, and allocated by region. Regional capital expenditures would be determined by a publicly accountable authority, using some measure of population-based need to aid in, and rationalize, the planning process. Hospital operating budgets could be set in various ways. One approach would be a simple global budget—based on past experience and anticipated new developments. Such a scheme could also vary what hospitals were paid if either more or fewer patients were admitted than anticipated. Alternatively, reimbursement could be based on the volume of admissions per diagnosis or procedure, more or less like the Medicare DRG system discussed in Chatper 3. Whichever approach was used, it would have to be designed to encourage the development of cost-reducing technology and overall operating efficienty. A system of "withholding" or rolling readjustments—similar to the one described for doctors—could be used to ensure compliance with expenditure limits.

If You Like the Post Office . . .

Opponents' primary criticism of the single-payer approach is that the political process is an inappropriate and unreliable method for deciding how much to spend on health care, or on the distribution of resources within the system. Governments, they say, are even more irrational than consumers. "Pork barrel" allocations and political payoffs would distort the health care system. They point to the obvious favoritism in everything from putting NASA headquarters in Houston to many state regulatory decisions on hospital construction as proof that this concern is well founded.

They also fear that such a process will constrain technological progress and reduce the amount of innovation in medical practice. Bureaucratic processes will tend to inappropriately limit payment for new treatments and strangle new investments. Current providers will be able to lobby all too effectively against potential competitors. Finally, managed competition's supporters express skepticism of any enterprise with such substantial public responsibilities. They just don't believe government will be able to play its role efficiently. "If you like the post office you will love government health care" is the slogan that embodies this point.

Single-payer supporters answer this last criticism by pointing to the Medicare system as an example of the federal government's competency at collecting and distributing money. Medicare's administrative costs are about 4 percent as opposed to those of private insurers, which average 14 percent. Admittedly, Medicare insures a very large group and does not have to spend money on marketing or underwriting. But neither would a single-payer system. Moreover, such a scheme would lower not only the administrative costs in the insurance industry (by largely eliminating that industry), but also the very substantial volume of those costs incurred by providers. Thus, much of the cost containment of single-payer schemes, supporters say, will come from cutting the administrative "tail" not the caring "tooth."

Single-payer advocates also argue that health planning can be superior to relying on the market provided it is done properly. Such planning, they say, will reduce costs, prevent duplication of services, ensure that equipment is fully utilized, and concentrate difficult procedures in regional centers, thereby ensuring higher quality from a skill perspective.

They point to Rochester, New York, where a cooperative, planned system has been in place for many years, as an example of what can be accomplished in this way. The health insurance industry in Rochester has been dominated by one insurer, since Blue Cross-Blue Shield had 70 percent of the market. This enabled long-term regional planning to occur. Perhaps even more important, the heavy involvement of the business community— led by a few large and progressive employers (i.e., Kodak and

Xerox)—has helped guarantee attention to the objective of containing health care costs.

As a result, the Rochester region has 3.1 beds per 1,000 residents, whereas New York State has 4.2 per 1,000 and the United States has 3.8 per 1,000. The investment in high technology has also been restrained—even with the presence in the area of a major medical school. Health insurance costs per employee in Rochester in 1991 were $2,378 versus $3,573 nationwide and $4,361 for the state of New York. Surveys also show that Rochester-area residents are more satisfied with their health care than adults nationwide.

Opponents of single-payer systems point out that in order to set adequate expenditure caps and muster the will and confidence to enforce them, accurate and timely data on service prices, service volume, outcomes, practice patterns, and quality must be available. A timely reporting system for all claims would need to be developed for volume performance standards to work effectively. Single-payer advocates respond that most of the same requirements would have to be met under managed competition. Any efficient system, whether market-based or regulated, will require better data on the outcomes and effectiveness of different treatments and providers than we currently have.

In sum, single-payer advocates point out that a major advantage of their approach is that managed competition is an unproved theory. A single-payer system, in contrast, demonstrably works in Canada. It may not be perfect or perfectly transportable, but it does work. And if we are going to reorganize the nation's largest industry, they claim that it would be nice to have that kind of assurance about the feasibility of our basic strategy.

Mixed Messages

While it might seem as if the single-payer and managed-competition theories are mutually exclusive, in fact that is not the case. There are a number of features of managed competition strategy which could move a plan some distance in the direction of a single-payer approach.

In particular, some argue that, "just in case," a managed-competition system should be combined with an expenditure cap. They argue that such a scheme would retain the advantages of market-based competition while also ensuring that total system expenditures did not rise above a fixed level. For example, each Health Alliance could be allocated a fixed amount per capita with which to negotiate.

Even some who are ambivalent about expenditure caps accept them on the pragmatic ground that they would help to sell the reform plan. Proponents of "pure" managed competition, however, dislike such a compromise. In their view, a global budget would undermine a basic feature of their approach—namely letting individual choice decide the overall level of society's health care expenditures. Some true single-payer advocates are also skeptical of such a mixed approach, arguing that capping premiums will only heighten the competition between plans to select the best risks. Other countries, they say, that have used global budgeting successfully, have done so with a high level of government involvement in allocating the budget among competing interests. Such involvement, which managed competition would lack, they argue, is central to getting the public to accept the results of the process.

Both sides acknowledge that under either system, implementing an expenditure cap would raise many additional issues. Who will determine these global limits, and their allocation, and by what process? What services will be included under the cap; all care or only those expenditures that are part of the standard benefit package? Will individuals be free to spend their own after-tax dollars on "luxury" medical care outside of any limits?

Tough problems of interregional equity will also arise in any national system—competitive or unified. Will historic geographic cost differences be preserved by the new arrangements, thus locking in Massachusetts to higher spending than, say, Kansas? Remember, under managed competition, the proposal is to set tax free contribution limits on the basis of the lowest bid in each region for the standard benefit package. Won't that procedure penalize citizens of regions that are the most efficient by limiting the tax benefits these citizens enjoy?

Another design decision that could push a managed-competition system toward the single-payer approach is the size threshold at which large employers will be allowed to arrange their own insurance. If all or almost all firms are forced into one Health Alliance, the Alliance itself begins to look more like a single-payer system, because most of the system's financing would come from a single source.

However, most larger companies are likely to fight hard to remain outside of any mandatory pooling and community-rating mechanisms in order to take advantage of their better loss experience. On the other hand, businesses with poorer than average health status will opt to be part of any larger pool. Allowing extensive opt-outs will thus risk re-creating the "adverse selection death spiral" of the current small business market in the larger Health Alliance risk pool.

A fourth key and contentious decision will be how to finance coverage. The more managed competition relies on equal per capita premiums, as opposed to payroll taxes, the closer it stays to the competitive ideal. On the other hand, one could imagine a scheme which, like Germany's, was financed entirely by payroll taxes—which the Alliance would pool and then pay out to insurance plans on a capitated basis.

This will be politically very sensitive since the more money that is raised by what looks like "premiums," the less that will have to be raised by politically objectionable "taxes." If everybody is in one Health Alliance, supported by "premiums" that are actually payroll taxes, much of the money raised to take care of the poor would not appear in the government budget. In contrast, if the cross-subsidy burden is placed only on those covered by a regional Alliance—the incentives for large employers to opt out of participating in such a scheme could become overwhelming. Thus, some added "tax" or "fee" on firms that remain outside the Alliance, or a scheme to deprive such plans of their tax deductible status, is a distinct possibility.

A final design decision is whether or not insurance coverage will actually be mandatory. Although the public perceives universal coverage to be an integral part of health care reform, some variations of managed competition would make coverage voluntary. Proponents of these plans believe that everything possible should be done to make insurance affordable and accessible, but that nobody should be forced to purchase coverage. In that spirit, they often support insurance regulation to prohibit preexisting condition exclusions and would offer various subsidies for low-income individuals and families. But quite a number of small employers, as well as conservatives suspicious of government, oppose employer and individual mandates on both economic and ideological grounds. They are particularly concerned that imposing added labor costs on small companies will detract from their ability to generate new jobs—which is an important function of the small business sector.

Supporters of a universal approach counter that the choice to be insured or not is illusory. In the United States today nobody actually gets left to die by the side of the highway. Emergency care for the uninsured is funded by a variety of cross subsidies within the health care industry, as well as by free care pools in various states. In most cases then, implicitly or explicitly, costs of caring for the uninsured are financed by "taxes" on the use of hospital care—through higher prices and premiums or through explicit surcharges on hospital bills. Those who opt for voluntary insurance purchases will thus be forced to continue to cross-subsidize emergency care for the uninsured through some such cost-shifting mechanisms. Supporters of a universal scheme believe it is preferable to have everyone contribute what they can, and not be "free riders" on the system.

The Past Is Prologue

Out of all this detail, we can see competing visions emerging about how to transform the American health care system. Those who would rely on market forces are not really upset at the growing "for-profit" orientation of doctors, hospitals, or insurance companies. They accept such motivation as inevitable and want to perfect and harness it—to make health care markets as competitive and cost conscious as the markets for automobiles or hamburgers.

Single-payer advocates, on the other hand, are disturbed at these developments. They want to rely more on professional judgment for priority setting, judgment disciplined by global resource limits set through accountable public processes. If, as a result, hospitals become less glamorous, if hospital CEOs get paid less, and the compensation of "high-roller" physicians decreases, they will not be displeased by such developments.

The risk to either plan is that whatever the Administration introduces into Congress will be barely recognizable when it emerges. Instead, it will undergo the George Bernard Shaw experience. Shaw likened being reviewed by the London theater critics to "being nibbled to death by ducks."

Suppose, as seems likely, managed competition comes to dominate the debate. As each interest group tries to mold the plan in its favor, the most controversial provisions will be those that will ensure universal access and control costs. And hence, these could be the first to be compromised. The result could easily be a plan that falls short of the fundamental restructuring of the system necessary to resolve our most pressing problems.

Now that we have set the context for the current debate and reviewed the major options, we also have to explore a whole set of detailed issues. It is, in a sense, amazing, how much remains to be decided even once a broad strategy is chosen. We discuss some of that in the next chapter before, in the last chapter, turning to what a good plan would actually look like. How will we know a good outcome if we are lucky enough to stumble across it amid the fog created by all the "blue smoke and mirrors" of the Washington debate? But first some "details."

6

DEALING WITH SPECIAL PROBLEMS

Enormous Details

Choosing an overall health care reform strategy will still leave many "details" unresolved—each of which is actually an enormously difficult policy dilemma. Eight such matters are explored in this chapter. First, reflecting its overall importance, is the link between health care reform and AIDS policy. As the nation's most serious communicable disease, AIDS throws into sharp relief many of the features of the "nonsystem" we have already discussed. Next, two areas, malpractice and prescription drug policy, are included because of their high-profile relationship to system costs. What is the extent of their contribution to overall costs and how do policies designed to control costs intersect with other policy concerns in these domains? Then, are three special problems of benefit design—what services should be covered in the health care reform package—that deserve discussion; namely mental health, dental, and long-term care. They raise, among other matters, the question of how we should think about what to include in any "standard benefit package." The chapter concludes with discussions of the education of physicians and of nonphysician health care workers. How will policy in those areas both affect and be affected by any reform effort?

Hammering out the policy "details" in each of these arenas is likely to be done by "experts" who are themselves interested parties—with much at stake in the outcome. But who else knows about the most promising opportunities for AIDS vaccines or the relative effectiveness of the care for various mental disorders, except those involved in the process? Thus, even in matters of "detail," it is necessary to explore each issue from a wider policy perspective. Otherwise, we run the risk of overly self-interested recommendations, a risk that was observable in some of the "working groups" that supported the Administration's Health Care Task Force last spring. Is it any surprise that a group of mental health professionals—whatever the merits of their case—recommended very generous mental health benefits?

AIDS: Ounces of Prevention and Pounds of Attempted Cure

Any health care reform effort will certainly have to confront the deeply troubling spread of AIDS. The disease now causes about 30,000 deaths per year—roughly comparable to the number caused by automobile accidents. Moreover, it has become the second leading cause of death among young males. The largest group infected so far has been—and perhaps 70 percent of the new cases continue to be—male homosexuals. The number of new cases, however, is increasing most rapidly among drug users, their sexual partners, and their children.

Ironically, but not surprisingly, the way the health care system has dealt with AIDS reflects many of its more general features and failures. First, we have spent much more on high technology—on both research and treatment—than we have on the much less glamorous activity of prevention. Second, many of those who are sick with AIDS are poor—and can neither pay for the high costs of their care, nor pay for actuarially "fair" insurance to cover those costs. Third, we have repeatedly had to confront the limits of our clinical knowledge. For example, recent carefully controlled clinical trials have shown that the early enthusiasm about the antiviral drug AZT may not have been warranted. Thus, neither a cure nor a vaccine can be counted on in the short run. The "techno-wizards" do not seem able to solve this one, at least not yet. Finally, as the epidemic has changed, we have had great difficulty redirecting our funding. In several metropolitan areas, entrenched groups have struggled over funding with newer organizations that are focused on those suffering from the more recent waves of the epidemic.

Part of the problem posed by AIDS is its geographic concentration. There are some areas (New York, northern New Jersey, and parts of Florida and California, as well as San Juan) that are, and will continue to be, especially hard hit. One recent study suggests that relatively comprehensive care will cost about $100,000 per case from infection to death. If we continue to rely on existing financing schemes, much of the cost of AIDS care will show up as increased outflows from bad debt and free care financing pools, or from Medicaid programs in these heavily affected states. To contain these costs, several states and programs have begun to make serious efforts to maintain AIDS patients outside of acute care hospitals.

But most of all, AIDS reveals our underattention to prevention and, therefore, the importance of adequately funding such efforts in any reform effort. To a certain degree, now that we know a great deal about the virus, it is not that difficult to protect oneself against AIDS. Avoid having unprotected sex or sharing drug injection paraphernalia with those infected with the HIV virus and one's risk is significantly controlled. But from a social policy perspective, widespread compliance with such precautions is easier to preach than it is to achieve.

Moreover, AIDS prevention reveals a deep difficulty encountered by many efforts aimed at behaviorally oriented prevention. The demands of program effectiveness and public acceptability may point in somewhat different directions. On one hand, programs designed to change behavior have to be persuasive to their target audience. On the other hand, the public—whose money is being spent—is understandably concerned about exactly what behavior is being promoted. Whether it is sex education in the schools, needle exchange programs, or encouraging safe sex, this dilemma has arisen repeatedly, and we can expect that it will continue to do so.

The need for enhanced prevention was underscored at the recent World Congress on AIDS. The news from researchers about vaccine development and antiviral drugs produced no great optimism. The virus mutates very rapidly and that fact alone greatly complicates vaccine development. Also, the virus can apparently "hide out" in various cells in the body—making it that much more difficult for the body's immune system to eliminate the infection.

And while it is not really part of what we're discussing in this book, I would be remiss if I did not point out that however great the AIDS problem is—or will become—in the United States, it is much more serious in many countries in Africa, Southern Asia, and Brazil. These nations have fewer health care resources and the loss of educated manpower to the disease, especially in some urban areas, could be quite devastating. Thus, it is not going to be enough to grapple with the question of what we owe each other, as citizens of the same nation, in the way of health care. AIDS is likely to force us to confront the even more confusing problem of our commitments and obligations to those abroad. In such places there are millions who are much less well off than even those who are relatively deprived in our own country.

Getting the "Mal" out of Malpractice

Next we turn to the question of medical malpractice and its relationship to health care costs. Few aspects of the current crisis have gotten such press attention. Malpractice produces good stories. Patients suffering serious injury, doctors paying incredibly high premiums, jury awards that rival a big win on the lottery: it all makes for a great two minutes on the evening news.

There are two possible links between the current system of malpractice law and health care costs. First, are physician fees higher because of the costs of malpractice insurance? And are those premiums, in turn, inflated by the frequency and exorbitant amounts of damage awards, as well as by high legal costs? Second, there is the issue of defensive medicine. How many extra tests and procedures do American doctors and hospitals undertake in order to protect themselves from possible malpractice litigation? In fact, neither of these claims can be supported empirically. Despite headline-grabbing premium levels in some high-risk specialties, overall malpractice premiums account for less than 1 percent of total health care expenditures. The magnitude of defensive medicine is harder to estimate—since it involves conjectures of what would happen under a system with different malpractice rules. Also, there are many other incentives in our system to do more—besides the threat of litigation. Yet, even the AMA, which has an interest in defending a high estimate, concludes from the available studies that defensive medicine, at most, contributes only 3 percent of overall health care costs. Moreover, neither of these is growing very rapidly, so they cannot account for recent cost increases.

Disposing of the linkage between malpractice and cost increases does not dispose of the problem of malpractice. There is still the issue of the amount of malpractice itself—and its link to the "skill" aspects of quality we reviewed in Chapter 4.

An extremely important study recently reviewed over 30,000 medical records of patients hospitalized in fifty-one hospitals in New York State in 1984. The analysis of these records revealed the following patterns:

- About 4 percent of all patients suffered "adverse effects" as a result of their medical care.
- In about one quarter of those cases, or in 1 percent of all hospitalizations, such events were the result of provider negligence.
- The incidence of adverse events, and of negligence, varied considerably among individuals. In general, poor, older, uninsured patients did worse, as did hospitals with predominantly minority patients.
- As few as one patient in fifty who suffered a negligent injury actually filed a malpractice claim, while only 20 to 40 percent of claims filed were for actually negligent events.

From a quality control viewpoint then, the current malpractice system is not working very well. There is a surprisingly high rate of medical injury. Moreover, our current "inspection" system is not working very well—the rates of both false positives (unsupported claims) and false negatives (valid unfiled claims) are very high.

This suggests that any reform plan should address the systems we use to control the general quality of medical care. The situation might be improved by making continuing medical education more effective and strengthening the state agencies—the boards of registration—that deal with professional discipline. It also seems likely that decreasing the frequency of actual malpractice should lead to fewer and smaller judgments—since the New York State study did find that, for all the imperfections in the system, the chances of being sued were higher when someone actually was negligent. Improving quality also means more than improving the performance of the worst performers. It should mean improving everyone's performance for the benefit of all patients in the system.

The steady improvement in the scientific basis of clinical practice, which has led to more standardized care and to a growth in the use of formal decision-guiding algorithms for physicians, should be viewed as a step in the right direction. These practices improve decision making and give physicians an effective defense under most state malpractice laws—which require doctors to meet "accepted standards of care."

It is also true that health care reform could facilitate malpractice reform, instead of the other way around. Under a comprehensive health insurance scheme, plaintiffs would no longer be able to claim that they needed large settlements to cover the future costs of care. Thus, the size of awards would be smaller, and premiums lower than they are today.

Various "tort-reforms" have been proposed to alter the system. The most radical idea is to move to a "no fault" basis— where only demonstration of injury would be required. Also radical is the notion of "enterprise liability," where health care organizations would be liable for staff errors. The intention of this proposal is to encourage hospitals to police their own physicians more stringently. A much less comprehensive proposal is to develop less expensive mediation processes to substitute for jury trials in some cases. Also an imposed limit on the size of "pain and suffering" awards has been reasonably successfully in several states. And these latter incremental improvements may be some-what helpful in holding down premiums. Still the data tell us that lapses on the part of providers are not randomly distributed. The old and the poor do receive worse care. That makes taking the "mal" out of "malpractice" noticeably more urgent.

Finding and Selling: Policy Toward Prescription Drugs

Another specific problem that has gotten a great deal of attention as a contributor to health care cost increases is that of prescription drug prices. From the *New York Times* to *Vogue,* the media have been full of stories about how U.S. drug prices are both too high for many to afford, and higher than those found in many foreign countries. Payments for drugs have been among the fastest growing components of health care spending. How-ever, such payments now account for only about 9 percent of health care costs, and thus cannot be a major driver of overall system cost increases.

Thus, the price of drugs may be more important from an access than from a cost perspective, a problem of affordability for certain individuals. Why, critics argue, should the same drug cost so much more in the United States than in Canada, Mexico, or Europe—where prices are 30 to 40 percent lower? In Mexico, prescriptions are not even required for most pharmaceuticals and a flourishing cross-border trade has grown up to service bargain-hungry American shoppers, some of whom save enough by stocking up on a year's supply of medication to pay for a week's vacation in the process.

The difficulties that arise in attempting to control the high prices for prescription drugs illustrate that these prices are not an accident. Instead, they are the perfectly predictable result of our efforts to encourage pharmaceutical research. As we noted in Chapter 2, the possibility of very high profits on the sales of a successful, patent-protected compound has been the prize we have used to lure private capital into funding drug research.

Moreover, in order for a compound to be successful, it has to be approved by the Food and Drug Administration. Under its governing legislation, the FDA has to review the drug for "safety" and "efficacy." The rules for that approval require an elaborate, time-consuming, and expensive multistage process—including carefully designed "double blind" clinical trials. The delay and cost of such studies only add to the profit levels companies seek to earn.

Perhaps less defensibly, high U.S. drug prices are also due to the advertising and marketing efforts of the drug companies. These expenses actually exceed the amount the pharmaceutical firms spend on research and development. The current system relies heavily on "detail men," who make individual sales calls on physicians, as well as on extensive advertising and often lavish promotional activities. One would be hard-pressed to find an American hospital whose employees don't all have "Tagamet" pens and "Tylenol" dispensers at their desks. In 1992, the pharmaceutical companies spent the equivalent of $25,000 per physician on marketing expenses.

In response to all these criticisms, there have been various drug policy innovations in recent years. Both prescribing practices and state laws have increasingly made it possible for patients to use "generic" substitutes for name-brand drugs when these are available. (Generic drugs are essentially identical drugs—without the original trade name—manufactured after a compound's patent protection has expired. The parallel is that many companies can now make copying machines—but only one can use the name "Xerox.") Similarly many health care organizations have developed "formularies"—lists of drugs approved for use. This is a way of limiting the use of expensive alternatives that do not offer meaningful performance advantages. Indeed, in some other countries even more aggressive price control efforts are in place, like the German "reference price" system which limits public payments for some drugs to the cost of least expensive therapeutic equivalent.

Concerned about possible government regulation, pharmaceutical companies have recently announced a series of measures designed to blunt public criticism. These include voluntary limits on the rate of price increases and programs to offer certain drugs at low cost to the poor.

One of the advantages of managed competition, according to its advocates, is that it would encourage provider groups to vigorously pursue such options. On the other hand, single-payer advocates argue that universal buyers would be even more effective negotiators with the pharmaceutical houses.

Similar to the malpractice issue, there are other aspects of drug policy besides cost control that are worth some close attention—in part because they intersect with our earlier discussion of AIDS. A number of AIDS activists have argued that the FDA rules for approving new drugs are too restrictive. Why wait for strong evidence of significant impact, they argue, if the patient's alternative is certain death? Defenders of the current system respond that it is important not to make new drugs available before clinical trials are performed. Otherwise, it will not be possible to recruit patients with critical conditions to participate in these trials. In a randomized trial, after all, not all of those enrolled actually receive the newest possible treatments.

Another way to put the same point is to realize, as I and others have argued elsewhere, that there are reasons to rethink the whole "safety" and "efficacy" approach to drug approval. Many drugs are efficacious exactly because they are *not* safe—because they have a powerful effect on the body. In fact, the whole idea that "safety" can be defined for strong medications is in itself misleading. Instead, the FDA should use the "reasonable option" standard: given its overall impact, good and bad, is a drug a "reasonable option" for certain patients? For someone who is dying, an "unsafe" drug—or even an unproven one—may be the best option, even if it does not meet the traditional approval standards.

This broad set of criticisms does not seem to have been falling on deaf ears. In practice, the FDA has moved in recent years to increase the flexibility of its procedures and has relaxed its criteria for AIDS drugs and similar compounds. But such changes should not blind us to the need for ensuring the continuation of well-designed clinical trials. The recent AZT studies remind us that clinical knowledge is difficult to come by and that the risks of self-deception are ever-present.

The central choice facing the nation is whether we want to continue to finance much of biomedical research by offering the lure of an enormous commercial jackpot—with the inevitable high prices and profits that such a policy entails. Or do we want to lower the size of that potential payoff in order to improve access to drugs? And if we do that, what impact will that have on the amount and direction of privately funded medical research around the world? While debate on these matters is quite appropriate, this brief review does suggest that pharmaceutical policy changes are, to some extent, separable from the broad strategic choices we face on health care reform. Thus, they need to be pursued on the merits, regardless of what is done more broadly.

Mental Health

Any health care reform effort will have to deal with the question of "benefit design." That is, exactly what services will it cover and to what extent. There are three areas we want to explore in this context, but none is more difficult, or more significant, than that of mental health services.

Mental illness is both widespread and also a significant cost to the society in terms of lost productivity. Many of these conditions first appear in adolescence or young adulthood and, in effect, become lifelong chronic disabilities. Looking only at major mental illness, studies suggest that between 2 and 3 percent of all adult Americans suffer from such conditions. Why, then, do insurance plans impose more restrictions on the amount of mental health care a patient receives than they impose on physical health services?

There are several conflicting considerations in any insurance benefit design decision. The most obvious services to include are those for which (1) demand is least influenced by price, (2) demand is least influenced by individual behavior, (3) there is high professional consensus on appropriate treatment, and (4) that treatment is generally effective. Covering services that meet those criteria is not likely to make a large impact on the amount of care individuals utilize. When one or more of these criteria are not met, insurance coverage tends to alter individual behavior, and/or insurers feel they are opening themselves up to unpredictable and uncontrollable costs.

Some believe that mental health services are a poor candidate for insurance because demand for such services is price sensitive and because of a lack of professional consensus on what care is effective. Thus, expanding coverage may encourage use, especially given the incentives to "overtreat" produced by volume-based compensation. Yet, such a simplistic analysis overlooks many of the complexities within this broad arena.

As far as effectiveness is concerned, as knowledge of the biology of mental illness has improved, the ability to treat a number of the most serious illnesses has expanded greatly (e.g., depression, panic, bipolar disorders, schizophrenia). That ability now compares favorably to what can be achieved in the way of symptom management and improved quality of life for many chronic physical conditions. Moreover, there is a high degree of professional consensus on how best to proceed in such cases.

The issue is less clear when it comes to dealing with the middle-class or working-class neurotic who is having trouble with child rearing or life-adjustment problems. Providing them with mental health care can easily be seen as a "luxury"—like cosmetic surgery—and an activity not deserving of public support. Yet in many of these cases, effective early intervention can in fact make a major difference in an individual's quality of life and even in long-run social costs (for schooling, criminal justice, and so on).

Many insurance plans have recently seen their costs skyrocket in this area—especially for drug and alcohol treatment. To control their costs, some plans restricted payment to inpatient settings—only to find to their dismay that the volume of beds devoted to such care immediately expanded. Thus, insurance companies worry that the very definitions of who is mentally ill and what constitutes mental illness are both unclear and expandable—at least around the edges.

Nor do the worries of insurance companies seem to be groundless. Some years ago the state of Texas removed controls on the construction of new inpatient psychiatric beds. As a result, several for-profit chains opened new facilities and the market in some metropolitan areas soon became overcrowded. In other words, these were too many beds and not enough patients. (This is, by the way, another clear example of the potential for competition to raise costs by producing surplus capacity.) As a consequence, professionals in some of these hospitals found themselves under pressure to make clinical observations that justified additional admissions or extended lengths of stay. There were also highly publicized fraud investigations in which hospitals were discovered to be billing insurance companies for impossibly intensive treatment in order to generate added revenue to cover high fixed costs with insufficient occupancy.

Insurance company anxiety about how to deal with mental health services is exacerbated by a lack of professional agreement as to who can appropriately offer services: psychiatrists? psychologists? social workers? psychiatric nurses? former addicts? clergy? Whenever any one professional group suggests that the members of another are an inappropriate source of care, there is immediate controversy. Are such credentialing requirements legitimate, or only a form of self-serving professional monopoly building?

The current patchwork system for financing mental health services is mind-boggling in its complexity. Much of this is the result of the movement to deinstitutionalize patients from public mental hospitals that began in the 1960s. During the 1970s and 1980s the number of beds in public mental hospitals decreased dramatically. Critical to those changes was the development of new drugs, especially the major tranquilizers and antidepressants—which allowed many individuals to function effectively in less restrictive settings. Financing also played a role as the states discovered that by closing state mental hospitals, and deinstitutionalizing the patients, they could shift much of the cost of supporting these clients to the federal government. One deinstitutionalized, these individuals become eligible for various federal disability benefits—which could be used to support community-based living situations. Moreover, once on disability support, such individuals were then eligible for Medicaid. Thus, when they did have to be hospitalized during acute episodes, the federal government paid half, provided they were cared for in psychiatric wards in general hospitals. In addition, there are a whole variety of federal grant programs which support various community mental health agencies that in turn offer service to clients.

One challenge to health care reformers will be to find ways to cover useful mental health services while not opening the door to the unlimited funding of less cost-effective care. To do that they obviously need to find practical ways to distinguish between the two—for example, by imposing high copayments on mental health visits to discourage questionable use. Decisions will have to be made about what to do about other existing mechanisms for publicly funding mental health care—and whether to try to incorporate that whole system into the AHPs and Health Alliances.

In making these decisions, we will repeatedly encounter a basic truism we noted at the very beginning of the book. As a society, we cannot afford all the care everyone would want at zero price. Any affordable system will involve some limits. The question, therefore, is not whether there will be limits, but which ones make the most sense.

Dental

Along with mental health, dental care has long been the poor relation of the American health care financing system. Most private insurance plans offer only modest coverage for dental services—such as coverage only for emergency injury repairs.

Dental health offers one of the clearest pieces of evidence concerning the impact of public financing on utilization by the poor. This can be seen by observing what did *not* happen to dental services—compared to hospital care—before and after the development of Medicaid. Before the program, the poor used much less than the rich in both areas. A few years later, however, the poor were using more hospital services (which were covered) than the rich. But their relatively lower use of dental services (which were not covered) had not changed very much.

Dental care also offers what is perhaps one of the greatest success stories in the field of prevention. Thanks to widespread fluoridation (and the introduction of fluoride toothpaste) the decline in dental cavities has been so great that it has significantly affected the income of dentists, the number in practice, and the enrollment in dental schools. Perhaps not surprisingly, dentists who remain in practice have sought to develop new services (like anticavity sealers) to help maintain their incomes.

Designing a sensible dental coverage policy raises many of the issues we have already encountered. First, how do we value quality-of-life benefits—including the psychological gains of cosmetic improvement—compared to the gains available from spending health care dollars in other ways? Second, to what extent can we afford to offer expensive but "nice to have" benefits to all—like elaborate orthodonture or restorative dentistry? If such services are not covered, of course, access to them will continue to be very different between rich and poor. Third, to what extent can we find ways to improve our preventive efforts even more? Fluoridation apart, minimizing the lifetime costs of dental care does depend critically on good old-fashioned individual behavior—brushing and flossing, etc.

Since insurance pays off when a policyholder suffers a loss, the presence of insurance can sometimes lead the insured to be less careful about avoiding injury. Economists worry about the possible effects of such incentives—termed "moral hazard." In health care the issue is complex since even if my insurance pays for my care, when I get sick I still suffer the symptoms of my disease. Thus I am not sure that "moral hazard" is really a problem for most conditions. Will I really be that much more likely to smoke if the care for my probably fatal lung cancer is government-financed? But it may be that changing the fiscal consequences of irresponsibility will influence dental prevention more than is the case for other conditions.

Finally, dental health raises in dramatic form the "backlog" problem that will trouble any transition to a more comprehensive health insurance system. Better insurance coverage, especially for outpatient care, will lead to increased contact with the health care system, which in turn will uncover a volume of unmet needs—especially in populations which previously had poor access. Thus short-run costs may be higher than long-run average costs—once the "backlog" has been dealt with.

In responding to such conditions, the country will repeatedly have to make choices about just how much to spend. There will be no easy or magic answer to these dilemmas. And while technical expertise can help clarify the options, ultimately it is social values that are really at stake.

Long-Term Care

Many of these same issues—as well as some additional ones—arise in relation to the third of our three benefit design issues, namely the coverage of, and the funding for, long-term care within a national health care reform plan. Because of increased life expectancy and the aging of the baby boom population, the number of people over sixty-five is expected to double by 2030; The over-eighty-five population—23 percent of which lives in nursing homes—is expected to more than double.

At one level, it might seem that acute care and long-term care could and should be separated. Yet that is not possible given the large role that Medicaid plays in funding nursing homes, and the burden of that funding on Medicaid budgets. Since almost any reform effort will involve Medicaid, the issue of how to treat long-term care will inevitably arise.

One way to think about "the long-term-care problem" is to consider how we as a society should provide and pay for the care, support, and housing of those of our elderly who are no longer able to function independently and who cannot pay for themselves. Put this way, this is not really a health care problem and still less a health insurance problem. Such expenses are highly predictable and a large part of them are for nonmedical goods and services.

Instead, the long-term-care problem involves two interconnected financing questions. First, how do we encourage individuals to engage in more savings during their productive years, so as to be able to support themselves later on. After all, the United States does have the lowest personal savings rate of any major industrial nation. Second, for those at lower income levels who cannot reasonably be expected to accumulate such savings, how do we finance their care?

Seen as a financing problem, it is clear that private insurance is not a solution. The insurance market offers little real risk spreading because of the extent of adverse selection. Most who buy policies expect to collect benefits in the near future. As a result rates have been quite high—high enough to discourage purchases by low-likelihood users. The amount of the premium for this coverage depends primarily on a person's age at the time of purchase and whether the policy covers future increases in health care costs. Thus, the small market for private long-term-care insurance functions as little more than a contractual savings plan.

The current system of utilizing Medicaid to finance long-term care is in need of reform. In many states, there are limits on eligibility connected to levels of personal assets. Thus senior citizens have to "spend down" to qualify. This means they face a choice between voluntary impoverishment or ineligibility. Potential Medicaid clients and their families can easily convince themselves that such rules are "unfair." Because many seniors have substantial equity in their homes, such resentment in turn fosters certain kinds of fraud, like dummy real estate transfers designed to evade the regulations. In response, some states have tried to change policy in various ways—for example by exempting some or all of residence values from eligibility determinations—but these have been far from universally successful.

In recent years, many states have also tried to alter the program's long-standing bias in favor of institutionalized care. Such care is often both more costly and less satisfactory to clients than home-care alternatives that allow seniors to maintain their existing locations and social networks. Yet home-care programs raise the possibility that expanding public spending will simply displace comparable private spending. The more capacity we create in publicly financed programs, the greater the utilization of such services will be. If services are sufficiently widespread, the incentives to save for old age will actually decline, especially if high asset levels are a bar to participation.

Relative to other industrial countries, the United States already has a high percentage of its elderly population in institutions. Whatever is done with regard to long-term care should not necessarily encourage this trend. Moreover, we clearly should not hold up the whole process of reforming the acute health care system—which itself will be so difficult—while we work on the complex social problems of who cross-subsidizes whom, and for what services, within the long-term-care arena.

Medical Education and Teaching Hospitals

The last two sections of this chapter deal with the problems of educating the work force. Such a discussion has to start with physicians—and the teaching hospitals that provide so much of their training—since it is doctors who make many of the key decisions about the nature and cost of health care.

One point is clear: the leverage of the government to manage the priorities of the education system is greatly diminished by the fact that so little of that education is publicly financed. For example, other countries use budgetary control to influence either the total supply of physicians or their distribution by specialty. The United States, in contrast, supports postgraduate medical education and teaching hospitals by means of automatic payments through the Medicare reimbursement system. This turns the decision making about what residency programs to offer over to the hospitals and the specialized medical societies that accredit such programs.

A second deleterious effect of the current system is the bias it induces away from primary care and toward specialized practice. In every other industrialized nation, 50 to 70 percent of the physicians are generalists. In the United States, the proportion of generalists has declined to less than 30 percent. In fact, less than 15 percent of medical students graduating in 1991 and 1992 intended to become generalists—meaning family medicine, pediatrics, general internal medicine, and obstetrics. As we saw in Chapter 3, all the fiscal incentives, as well as much of the socialization pressure, point students in this direction. Indeed, the political legitimacy of government—when it comes to limiting physician income or redeploying doctors into less lucrative practice patterns—is substantially diminished by the very high sums doctors have to pay for their education. For that financial burden provides an obvious justification for doctors' current choices, and for their resistance to any efforts at change.

While full-scale public financing of medical education is very unlikely, there is growing support for a plan to help students with medical school costs in exchange for a certain number of years of service in underserved areas. This could be done, for example, with a tuition loan-plus-forgiveness program. Many details of such a plan would have to be worked out. Would it be open to all, or would it favor certain specialties or students who themselves come from underserved areas? How much service time would be required for how much forgiveness? And how do we make sure the doctors actually follow through in their commitments? But if such a scheme were in place it would not only help redistribute physicians, but could also make other kinds of reforms easier to accomplish.

If we were to expand the public role in medical education, we might well find that we have an oversupply of medical school training capacity from the perspective of a sensible health care system. In 1975, we had roughly one physician for each six hundred citizens. We now have approximately one for each four hundred and this ratio is projected to shrink even further in the years ahead. Moreover, data suggest that one possible cause of inappropriate care, especially excess surgery, can be physician supply. In one study the strongest predictor of per capita surgery rates in a region was the per capita number of surgeons.

Ironically, medical school application rates have begun to increase, after some period of decline. However, the poor economy generally and a decline in the prestige of business (as a result of various recent scandals) are also causing that trend. And in any case, the scope of our training system should be tied to the size of the medical care system the country can support, not to the career aspirations of the current crop of twenty-two-year-olds. Indeed, the increased demand for medical school admissions should reassure policymakers. It suggests that reforms which would slow the growth of physician incomes will not necessarily undermine the supply of capable students wanting to pursue medical careers.

The problems of finding ways to support the major teaching hospitals are, however, even more difficult. As we noted in Chapter 3, these hospitals have especially high costs—roughly twice that of community hospitals—in part because they support a substantial part of the costs of postgraduate medical education through patient care revenue. Moreover their favorable treatment within the Medicare reimbursement system has been critical to their continued fiscal health.

These institutions might have a tough time under certain forms of managed competition. Provider networks will have every incentive to treat patients in the lowest-cost hospitals, and use the teaching hospitals only for the most difficult cases. The recent expansion in the number of physicians will only make such shifts easier to undertake. In many areas, there are a growing number of young, well-trained specialists practicing outside of university hospitals. As a result, such hospitals are able to compete with the teaching centers across an increasingly sophisticated spectrum of services.

Thus, managed competition just might force us to find other mechanisms for funding teaching hospitals besides the current system of paying them by means of increased prices for patient care. These hospitals have long resisted such an alternative. They claim that direct government funding would open them up to increased government influence over their priorities and activities. The counterargument is that such influence might not be all bad. The teaching hospitals' view reminds me of a famous statement by the GM executive and later Secretary of Defense Charles Wilson. When asked if he saw any possible conflict of interest between his company's gain and the interests of the nation he replied, "For years I thought what was good for our country was good for General Motors, and vice versa. . . ." Yet in fact, what looks best from the perspective of an institution may not always best serve the system. Hence, some increased public influence might be appropriate.

Moreover, what will happen if the training of physicians does shift more toward primary care and the use of outpatient settings? It might then turn out that there is a surplus of postgraduate medical education capacity in certain regions or specialty areas—not to mention a surplus of beds in the most high-tech hospitals. Indeed there are already some teaching hospitals where lower admissions have led to more residents in training than there are patients. Thus, a somewhat painful downward readjustment in this sector is a distinct possibility.

The Supply of Nonphysician Health Care Workers

Critics of American education have recently focused on the poor performance of our system in training people for technical jobs at a level below that of the four-year college or university. This is especially striking in comparison, say, to Germany, with its elaborate and well-developed apprenticeship system. Such an educational failure has social as well as economic implications. A well-trained technical work force is obviously vital to cost-effective production in many sectors. But such training is also critical for helping many advance up the social and economic ladder. And as the largest industry in the economy, health care is an obvious candidate to play a role in this process.

Yet, unfortunately, the health care sector reflects many of the general inadequacies of American technical education. For example, in many specialized areas like radiology or laboratory technicians, there have been persistent shortages. And yet relatively few institutions have stepped forward to provide the training capacity to fulfill these needs.

In this context, it is also worth noting the special problems of nursing supply. Nurses go to school in a variety of settings. Nearly two thirds receive their basic RN education in associate degree programs at community colleges. A declining fraction—about one third the remainder (mainly in the East)—train in what was the traditional setting, namely hospital-based diploma schools. And the rest go through four-year Bachelor of Science in Nursing programs. However, a good number of associate degree nurses eventually go on for B.S. degrees. And there is an increasing number of advanced practice nurses, serving as clinical specialists, nurse practitioners, or nurse midwives, who have received master's degrees.

At the opposite end of this occupational spectrum, many hospitals employ some workers with less training and fewer skills to help RNs with selected less technical tasks. Some of these workers are LPNs or LVNs—two equivalent terms (which stand for licensed practical nurse and licensed vocational nurse) that are used in different regions of the country. There are also a variety of job titles like nurses' aide or nursing assistant in various states or institutions.

One of the challenges to health care reformers is to find ways to organize care so that workers with various levels of skill and education can play appropriate roles within the health care system. For example, what tasks can advanced practice nurses or physician assistants perform more cost-effectively than can physicians themselves? Similarly, how can we organize systems of training so that individuals can progress from job to job as they complete additional education? Finding ways to do this may be critical for allowing individuals from less advantaged backgrounds and with fewer resources to finance their own progress up the occupational ladder.

As we pursue such changes, however, we should also be wary of allowing ourselves to re-create (or perpetuate) the sort of "two-class" medicine that has so often been characteristic of American health care. On the one hand, limitations on the practice of nonphysicians that are not warranted for quality reasons are clearly irrational. All they serve to do is to defend the status and income of the physicians whose monopoly they protect. On the other hand, rational licensing and practice rules can serve valid consumer protection and quality-control purposes. A system in which we have doctors for the middle class and other practitioners for the poor is thus open to certain equity objections.

Ironically, but understandably, many health care professionals seem to believe that limits on practice make sense when they serve to protect their own turf from others with lesser training, but are unfair or irrational when they restrict their own role. Doctors, for example, often want to defend their roles by limiting nursing practice, but criticize efforts by nurses to do the same for their functions—while the nurses take exactly the opposite view. The debates about practice roles in mental health, among psychiatrists, psychologists, and other would-be therapists, have exactly the same structure. And then there are the optometrists, podiatrists, chiropractors, etc. What is required is a rethinking of such rules not from the perspective of any one of the various provider groups, but from the viewpoint of what will provide cost-effective access to quality care for all groups in society.

Conclusion

By now the reader may well be overwhelmed with all the detail and complexity. But in a sense that has been my purpose in this chapter. An effective response to the health care crisis requires more than endorsing a few broad principles. There are innumerable interlinked details to consider. How we deal with those details will say a lot about how any reform effort will ultimately impact all of our lives. With that sobering thought in mind, we can turn to our very last topic. What in fact is likely to happen and how should we evaluate the results of any reform effort?

7

BACK TO THE FUTURE:
The Vision of Health Care Reform

How Do We Think About All This?

What is the best way to conclude a book like this? With a summary of major points? Too long, repetitive, boring, and detailed. With a prediction? Too likely to be proven incorrect. Instead, I propose to conclude by taking a cue from the "back to the basics" movement in education. What exactly is *basic* to our national vision for the health care system? What is it that we actually would like to do? Even more basic than that, how should we think about what would make for a desirable system?

Again and again, the analysis in this book has illustrated that critical value choices are embedded in health policy decisions. Responsible health care reform will require us to consider more than our individual private gain—although doing that is certainly a legitimate part of the process. We also need to consider what would constitute a fair and durable set of arrangements for the society as a whole. Participating in the political process is not the same as going to the mall. Congress is not some grand Wal-Mart store where all we do is hunt for the best bargains for ourselves. Voting is not like shopping—or at least it should not be.

Unfortunately, the American public is stuck at the developmental stage of early adolescence when it comes to economic policy. Thirteen-year-olds want what they want. They don't want to be told that if they go out with their friends, they won't have time to finish their science project. Instead, they get angry with the "messengers" who bring them the bad news about their limited options. The deficit reduction debate in 1993 revealed this pattern far too clearly. Everyone wanted lower taxes, a lower deficit, and no cutback in their favorite program! Import the same attitude into the health care reform debate and we could be doomed from the start.

The point of departure we should use then is *not* simply "What is best for me?" Citizens in a democracy are, to some extent, agents for the society as a whole. When we choose a health care system we are not only making decisions for ourselves, but for everyone else in the country as well. We will all have to consume/enjoy/suffer the same systems of hospitals, taxes, insurance companies, research incentives, and medical schools. "Citizen" is itself an important public office in a democracy, and as such it carries with it certain public responsibilities.

But then how should we think about what to choose? The eminent political and moral philosopher John Rawls has proposed a particular thought experiment that he claims correctly frames the question. He calls his conceptual device "the original position." His idea is to ask, "What set of social arrangements would each of us choose if we did not know who in the world we would become?" This means not knowing anything about ourselves—including our age, tastes, our health status, or our values. Only in this way, says Rawls, can we choose general social principles which are truly fair to all.

Few ideas have been more hotly debated in the academic philosophy community over the last twenty years than Rawls's proposal. The result has been a rich, highly nuanced, and often relentlessly esoteric debate in the course of which Rawls and some of his followers have decided that various specific matters—including health care—are too complex and detailed to be settled by means of his basic technique. However, one point has emerged from that conversation which is relevant to the counter-proposal I am about to offer. It is difficult, if not impossible, to think about what we would prefer if we did not know who we are and what we actually value. The best we can do is think in the ways that we think, and choose in response to our own deepest convictions and intuitions—honed and developed by our experience in thinking and choosing.

So we have to think about choosing a health care system in a way that reflects our actual views and values. But how can we do that in a way that also takes account of our views about fairness and social responsibility—in a way that does justice to our roles as citizens?

This is where the "Generative Position" comes in. The term comes from Erik Erikson's analysis of the human life cycle. The "generative" stage of life is the time in later middle age when we begin to worry about the longer run, about the world that our children and grandchildren will inherit. The "Generative Position" asks each of us to imagine ourselves as the agent for future generations. Suppose all future members of the society were our children and grandchildren?

The question for the reader is then, "What kind of health care system would *you* design if you were trying to act as an honest agent on behalf of everybody?" Remember, think about the problem as if *everyone* were your child, including those who have to pay the premiums or the taxes, those who work as nurses or doctors, and those who are poor and in need. To what extent do you want access to health care to depend upon individual income? How much spending on health care is enough, or too much, given competing goals and "opportunity costs"? Is it more important to you that when your children get to be age eighty-six there will be unlimited resources available to prolong their lives to age eighty-eight, or that your children not suffer from some preventable disability that limits their capacity during the prime of their lives?

Seven Specific Questions

For me, one way to use the "Generative Position" to make sense of the policy morass is to try to formulate the major concerns and values that emerge from such an analysis as the questions to which health care reform is the answer. Instead of starting with questions, most policy advocates follow the "Carnac the Magnificent" principle and start with answers. Carnac, the Johnny Carson character, did likewise. He always intuited the answer before he revealed the question.

Instead I propose to proceed in a spirit that is the opposite of the Carnac approach. Here are seven questions that I believe should be asked of any reform proposal if we are to take the perspective of the "Generative Position" seriously. They are presented unnumbered, so that readers can consider relative importance on their own. If a plan does not provide real progress on most of these points, the larger question, "Why bother?" is certainly very much in order.

UNIVERSALITY
■ Will the plan provide for universal, portable coverage for a reasonable array of health care expenses without exclusions for preexisting conditions?

EQUITY
■ Will the cost burden of such coverage be distributed in a way (whether through taxes, premiums, or service fees) that fairly reflects individuals' ability to pay?

COST CONTROL
■ Will there be effective cost-control mechanisms that limit overall health care spending—and do so in a way that tends to eliminate low-productivity expenditures?

EFFICIENCY
■ Will the plan encourage the right internal changes in the system, that is, will it foster efficient institutional reorganization, end duplication and overcapacity, and diminish administrative costs?

ACCESS/QUALITY
■ Will it facilitate uniform access to high-quality services regardless of social or economic circumstances or personal characteris-

tics—where quality is defined by skill, appropriateness, and caring?

CHOICE
■ Will a reasonable degree of consumer choice be preserved so that individuals can choose, and change, the doctors they deal with?

PREVENTION
■ Will the new arrangements help shift resources into preventive measures, to lower the burden of disease to begin with?

Notice, this formulation does not fully accept the current popular formulation—namely, that premiums and/or out-of-pocket costs are "too high." The real issue is more complex. Is the system efficient and are costs fairly allocated? Obviously, many of the critical terms used in these questions are ambiguous. What is a "reasonable" scope of covered services, or a "fair" distribution of fiscal burdens? Clearly, the all-important detailed meaning of those terms has to be worked out in the political and administrative process by which any plan is first chosen and then becomes reality.

Three Major Obstacles

What stands between America and the development of a health care system that offers us positive answers to these questions? I believe that there are three major obstacles: self-serving politics, limited imagination, and insufficient empathy.

By *self-serving politics* I mean the current scheme in which personal advantage and partisan point-scoring seem to have become the primary goal in the Washington game. And as a force shaping how that game is played we cannot ignore campaign financing—which does so much to increase the influence of economically powerful interests. For we have to face the fact that major gains will require major changes. For example, if we are to control costs, we will have to either eliminate the incentives for doctors to do more, or at least limit their capacity to generate unlimited costs by doing so. In many hospitals, the mahogany-paneled executive offices, glass and marble public spaces, and top-heavy administrative structures (in both numbers and compensation)—all could, and perhaps should, be casualties of a serious reform effort. And then there is the prospect of either eliminating or at least transforming much of the health insurance industry! As one commentator once put it, "We need to find productive jobs for all of those medical underwriters."

Does the public fully understand that the screams of protest from those interest groups whose financial stakes are highest might in fact be a sign that reform efforts are actually on the right track? And perhaps the righter the track, the louder the screams? Are we prepared for the self-serving press releases, the exaggerated claims, the scare tactics, and possibly even the outright lies, that these groups and their "hired guns" in Congress will offer up at every available television interview opportunity?

For we have been through this before. In the early days of environmental regulation, business organizations and the EPA regularly disagreed on the likely costs of various control programs. Yet, after the fact, it often turned out that even the EPA's lower cost estimates were too high. The manufacturers' estimates always, always, were far too high—just perhaps because they had every strategic reason for making such mistakes.

The challenge to leaders of both parties will be to exhibit genuine leadership and to do so by honestly explaining our real options and their very real implications. The public must be urged to make the tough choices, instead of avoiding them and sinking further into the quicksand of the swamp. Saying—as one Republican senator did last summer—that he was in favor of universal coverage but against employer mandates and yet could not, or would not, offer other suggestions about how to finance coverage surely does little to advance public understanding. Too often in Congress, partisanship takes over and members seem motivated by the goal of preventing the "other side" from being able to claim a victory—even if they have to contribute to policy gridlock and public infantilism in the process. It could be that the public's vision of the future, and of the necessary steps to get us there, is *bolder* than our politicians give us credit for. While they are mired in partisan arguments, we confront the consequences of their timidity in our daily lives.

The second major obstacle is the way in which a *limited imagination* prevents us from seeing even our own self-interest clearly. Too many of us look at the health care system, and its deep inherent flaws, and believe that we can save ourselves by tinkering around the edges. Why should I, as a worker, support a universal system since I now have a good job with benefits? (Will you always?) Why should I, as a business executive, get involved in controlling system costs, since my company's plan costs less than what my competitors pay? (What about potential competitors abroad?) Why should we, as members of the middle class, spend money on prevention since "those people" bring their ills on themselves? (Who will pay for their care and their social services in the long run?)

The point is that many features of a well-designed national system make good self-interested sense for many in the middle class. Yes, they might pay higher taxes, but their insurance premiums could go down and their wages could go up more than enough to make up for that. Yes, under a single-payer system doctors might find their incomes more limited—but they also might gain enormously from decreased insurance company micromanagement. Yes, senior citizens might lose their own special funding if Medicare is wrapped into a new program, but their out-of-pocket costs might be less and their benefits more secure if a unified system allowed us to bring overall system costs under better control. But seeing these indirect and longer-run gains from reform will take some imagination.

Finally, there is evidence of *insufficient empathy*. We have repeatedly encountered the inequalities of the American health care system. Those toward the bottom of the socioeconomic spectrum experience less access to surgical procedures, more frequent victimization by provider negligence, less effective caring in hospitals, higher infant mortality rates, and shorter life expectancies. We have stressed that some of these phenomena reflect inequities that far transcend the medical care system. But many of them reflect inequalities at the very heart of that system.

Moreover, much of this inequality is the result of not having a universal system. It is difficult enough to overcome the social barriers to equitable access. But a fragmented system with varied reimbursement makes it almost impossible to achieve that goal.

Individuals who are socially marginalized discover that providers treat them reluctantly because they are uninsured, or covered by a cost-constrained public system that pays lower fees. Working Americans with sick children lie awake at night wondering about how to trade a visit to the doctor against the food or clothing budget. The comfortable elite, to which all the "usual suspects" and their official audience in Congress and the Executive Branch belong, don't always seem to understand just how frightening the "your money or your life" choice is when someone has to make it for real.

Representative Fortney "Pete" Stark tried to make this point in an imaginative way. He proposed that every member of Congress be required to enroll in the lowest-bidding health plan in the member's district. His point was that market fragmentation will undermine empathy and reinforce inequality, since the policymakers won't share the experience they impose on others.

Along these lines, I am reminded of an airline strike in the Eastern states and a simultaneous nationwide Greyhound bus strike perhaps twenty-five years ago. Congress immediately invoked the Taft-Hartley Act to get the airlines flying—saying it was a major national emergency. The bus strike dragged on for many weeks without intervention. In fact, the buses carried more people and freight than the relevant airlines—but no congressmen on their way back to their districts.

Just Do It!

It is tempting to think that imposing health care reform will be a little like carrying through on a new exercise program, that the task, in the words of the Nike commercial, is to "Just do it!" But that is not really the case. Instead, it will depend on whether or not the vision we embrace is really carried out with enough vigor and internal consistency to have any hope of success.

Managed competition in particular is often profoundly misunderstood because it seems like, and is sometimes presented as, mere incremental reform that builds on our existing system. Yet in some ways, it is by far the more radical option. True, it will save the insurance industry (after all, the largest insurers call themselves "the Alliance for Managed Competition"). But it will force a greater transformation of the health care industry than the single-payer alternative. Single-payer seeks to reorganize the financing and insurance function—which in many ways is the part of the health care system individuals see less of. Managed competition seeks to reorganize not only the financing system and the insurance market, but the whole care-giving process as well. Exactly because a single-payer system would be less disruptive to the care-giving process, it might be more acceptable to many physicians. Surveys reveal that what physicians would object to most in a new national health plan are increased paperwork, hassle, and micromanagement, and salaried employment. They apparently would accept fee-for-service payments from a fixed budget under an expenditure cap, and even lower compensation for themselves, if they could reduce interference in their practices in the process.

In any case, the interested parties will have every incentive to "stick it out" and influence the implementation process once the first great enthusiasm for any reform effort has begun to fade. Many state efforts at health care reform, in recent years, have encountered exactly this difficulty. A law is passed, but then implementation suffers as the interests mount a successful counterattack. Massachusetts passed legislation with an employer mandate to achieve universal coverage—but the start of the program has been repeatedly postponed. Kentucky passed a similar plan—but the governor had to settle for a study commission once it became clear that the state confronted the need to either impose an employer mandate or raise new taxes. A commission in Vermont was asked to prepare both a managed-competition plan and a single-payer plan for the legislature to consider—but didn't design a real single-payer option because it didn't want to confront the insurance reorganization and tax implications of such a scheme.

Indeed, the experience of Hawaii, which has the only existing employer mandate scheme in operation in the United States, is very instructive in this regard. The Hawaiian requirement came very early—in 1974—in a state with a buoyant economy, where insurance coverage exceeded 90 percent, where there were only two insurance companies (one was an HMO), and where there were the fewest hospital beds in the nation. As a result of these and other factors, costs, utilization, and health outcomes in Hawaii look more European than American. And a vibrant small business sector has created many jobs in a service-oriented economy despite any inhibiting effects the mandate might have had. But Hawaii was admittedly the "best case" situation for actually implementing such a mandate—in part because it did so little to disturb existing power relationships.

In recent decades, there have been many studies of the operation of government programs—whether they involve planning, regulation, financing, or direct service functions. Two important implications emerge from these. First, the actual language of a law, or a regulation, is often ambiguous when applied to a particular case. The world is typically far too complicated—it contains too many gray areas—for the language we use to sort it into clearly defined categories. What technology is "feasible"? What constitutes "a good faith effort"? Not to mention, how "safe" is "safe" or how "fireproof" is "fireproof." As a result, there is almost always a substantial amount of discretion in the implementation process. Second, the way in which agencies utilize that discretion reflects a whole series of managerial decisions: recruitment, training, rewards, task divisions, communication patterns, supervisory leadership, etc.

Thus the full meaning of any reform will be uncovered only when it is implemented. This means that we had best design systems and processes that are "robust"—that can be implemented by real, imperfect human beings with real mixed motives, limited intellectual capacities, and only partial insight. Evidence that a proposed process has actually worked somewhere in the world, that a particular arrangement has functioned as intended, that some experience makes a specific prediction plausible: these are things we should take seriously in our policy choices.

One particularly important implementation issue will involve just how much flexibility we give the states to develop their own plans. It seems reasonable that state flexibility should be concentrated on implementation details as opposed to fundamental goals. As in Medicaid, there should be federal standards to meet—with a waiver provision to allow some administrative discretion. The Canadian system is like that—with substantial provincial discretion and responsibility for implementation. There are reasons, however, to ensure that a significant part of the financing of any scheme has a national base. Otherwise states with more health risks—which are correlated to social and economic problems—will face higher costs. And states will then be tempted to compete for industrial development by trying to deprive the disadvantaged of care. That result would hardly constitute "national" health care reform.

The Possibilities for Pride

Is it possible to transform the politics of health care reform, and through such a process achieve a better result? The experience in Oregon in recent years is actually a hopeful model in this regard. Led by State Senator John Kitzhaber, who is also a physician, the legislature in Oregon passed an imaginative plan to create a system of universal, yet limited, coverage. Everyone would be included, but procedures would be rank-ordered on a list and those that provided the least gain for the money would not be paid for.

There ensued a several-years-long process of study commissions, technical reports, hearings, public meetings around the state, task forces, plan revisions, and so on. The initial priority list was criticized as overvaluing quality-of-life gains versus lifesaving. The Bush administration refused to give the state a waiver from the Medicaid law to conduct its experiment. The state legislature procrastinated on funding the plan. And incentives to encourage employers to voluntarily expand coverage have not produced the desired effect. Yet through the terms of two governors, the effort has gone forward, clearing successive obstacles. The state now has its waiver. The legislature decided on a financing plan. And whatever one thinks of the specifics of the Oregon approach— the honesty and explicitness of the public debate are both a challenge to those in Washington, D.C., and a positive sign that democratic deliberation about health care may actually be possible.

I happen to be a hockey fan. And one of the television commentators for the Boston Bruins, the former player Derek Sanderson, has a way of putting this point very well. When the team is playing without real energy, Derek will say, "Everyone is waiting for George to do it. But George didn't lace up his skates tonight. Someone on the ice will have to pick it up." This will be the ultimate challenge to citizens when it comes to national health care reform. The citizens of America are "the team on the ice" when it comes to this issue. It is just possible that our political leadership underestimates the capacities of that team. Do we have the imagination, the empathy, and sense of civic responsibility to create a system all Americans can truly be proud of? We will see.

A GLOSSARY OF "HEALTHSPEAK":
Buzzwords You Need to Know

- **Accountable Health Plan or AHP** (sometimes Accountable Health Partnership) Organizations that would combine health insurance and care-giving functions. They could function much like an HMO but could also be more loosely organized networks.

- **Adverse Selection** Process whereby individuals who know they are most at risk of having an insurance claim disproportionately purchase insurance.

- **AFDC or Aid to Families with Dependent Children** Usually called welfare, this is a joint federal-state program that provides grants to those low-income individuals and their dependent children who meet eligibility criteria.

- **Alliance for Managed Competition** A lobbying organization begun by the major health insurance companies.

- **Ambulatory Care** Care provided to individuals who are not inpatients in a health care institution.

- **Ambulatory Care Sensitive Condition** Medical conditions for which hospitalization can be significantly decreased with effective ambulatory care.

- **American Hospital Association or AHA** A trade association that represents most hospitals in the United States. The organization operates mainly through various state associations.

■ **American Medical Association or AMA**   An association devoted to protecting the interests of American physicians. Currently only 39 percent of U.S. doctors are dues-paying members.

■ **Bad Debt and Free Care**   Hospital bills which are not paid. Free care refers to the bills of those too poor to be expected to pay. Bad debt refers to bills left unpaid by those who reasonably might be expected to pay.

■ **Blue Cross**   An association of statewide nonprofit insurance companies that cover hospital costs. Started by the American Hospital Association, the "Blues" have often received favorable rates from hospitals.

■ **Blue Shield**   An association of nonprofit insurance plans for covering physician expenses. Now merged with Blue Cross in most states.

■ **CABG or Coronary Artery Bypass Graft Surgery** (often pronounced "cabbage")   A procedure in which a vein from the leg is attached to one or more coronary arteries, bypassing obstructions in those arteries, to enhance blood flow to the heart.

■ **CalPERS** (pronounced cal-pers)   Stands for the California Public Employees Retirement System, which purchases health insurance for government employees, retirees and dependents in California.

■ **Cardiac Catheterization**   A process for taking detailed X-ray images of the blood vessels leading to the heart. A thin tube is inserted in the leg so that various compounds that show up clearly on X-rays can be injected into the blood vessels in question.

■ **Chief of Service**   Many hospitals are organized into distinct services—corresponding to the different specialties. Each such service typically has a chief. In a small community hospital, these individuals will often be non-salaried. There may only be two services, medicine and surgery. A major teaching hospital will have twenty service chiefs—each also a professor at the affiliated medical school.

■ **Chronic Condition**   A condition that persists over time. Usually used in opposition to an acute or emergent condition.

∎ **Clinical Trial** A carefully conducted study of the effectiveness of a new medical drug, device, or treatment. Such trials often rely on "random assignment" and can be "double blind."

∎ **COBRA** (pronounced "cobra") The Consolidated Omnibus Budget Reconciliation Act of 1985 requires employers to make it possible for individuals who lose their health insurance for various reasons to continue to purchase such coverage for two years with their own funds, through the employer's plan.

∎ **Commercial Insurance** Refers to insurance purchased through a for-profit commercial insurance company—in contrast to insurance purchased through Blue Cross.

∎ **Community Rating** Setting health insurance rates so that everyone in the community pays the same rate. Some forms allow modest adjustments for age and sex. The opposite of "medical underwriting" or "experience rating."

∎ **Co-payment** A fee that has to be paid by health insurance customers when they use health care—despite their insurance. Such "co-pays" range from nominal fees per visit (say $3.00 at an HMO) to 10 percent or 20 percent of all costs up to some pre-set limit.

∎ **CT Scan or CAT Scan** Stands for "computer tomography" or "computer-aided tomography." Such machines use multiple X-ray exposures from different angles, processed by a computer, to construct an image superior to a conventional X-ray.

∎ **Death Spiral** When "adverse selection" gets out of control and sets off successive waves of rate increases. At each stage the healthier subscribers drop their insurance because it has become too expensive—and only those who know they will need it (i.e., those who are sick) retain coverage.

∎ **Deductible** Annual expenses a subscriber has to pay before an insurance plan covers health care costs. These often apply to a subscriber and his or her family in total.

∎ **Defensive Medicine** Performing or ordering tests or procedures that would not have otherwise been performed, in order to be able to defend against a malpractice claim.

■ **Diminishing Marginal Returns** An economics concept which says that additional resources devoted to producing any output eventually become less effective and so produce less output. This phenomenon explains "flat of the curve" medicine.

■ **Direct Teaching Cost Adjustment** A payment to a teaching hospital made by the Medicare program that covers the actual costs of supporting the teaching function.

■ **DRG or Diagnostic Related Groups** System used by Medicare for paying hospitals and now widely used by other payers as well. A hospital is paid a fixed fee for each admission—the fee is set separately for each of over 400 diagnostic categories. There are also special adjustments for expensive ("outlier") cases.

■ **Eligibility** Rules governing who can be covered by a public health insurance program. Eligibility for Medicare is based on age. Eligibility for Medicaid depends on the individual being eligible for another government program like AFDC or SSI, or other criteria.

■ **Employer Mandate** The requirement that all employers offer health insurance to their employees—with the employers covering some specified fraction of the cost. In some schemes, employer costs would be capped at a specified fraction of their payroll costs. Hawaii is the only state which currently has such a requirement.

■ **Enterprise Liability** A plan for reforming malpractice law which would make the organization a doctor works for liable for any malpractice claims. The idea is to make that organization do what is necessary to select, train, and supervise doctors in order to avoid malpractice.

■ **ERISA** (often pronounced "ah-riss-ah") Employee Retirement Income and Security Act of 1974. This federal law exempts many employer- and employee-run health and welfare plans from state regulation. As a result it encourages large employers to "self-insure."

■ **ESRD** A funding program for End Stage Renal Disease under Medicare that pays for kidney dialysis and kidney transplants.

■ **Experience Rating** Setting health insurance rates for a large group based on their own actual health care expenses. Allows healthier employee groups to pay less for their insurance.

▪ **Failures of Success** One result of a successful medical care system is to increase the number of individuals in a society who are alive but partially or totally disabled by their medical condition.

▪ **Family Physician (also Family Practice)** A specialty designed to take the place of general practice. Such physicians—who also do both pediatrics and obstetrics—have frequently been recruited to work in rural and underserved areas.

▪ **Fee for Service** Refers to the practice of paying physicians on the basis of the services they perform—as opposed to having them be on salary.

▪ **Flat of the Curve Medicine** Medical care that produces relatively little or no benefit for the patient as a result of "diminishing marginal returns."

▪ **Formularies** Lists of approved drugs that are the only ones that can be prescribed by physicians participating in the program. The list generally excludes more expensive options when cheaper, equally effective drugs are available.

▪ **FTE or Full-Time Equivalent** A way of measuring the staffing level of a hospital. Since many hospital workers work part-time, their hours are combined to calculate the number of employees that there would have been if all work had been done by those working full-time.

▪ **Fully Allocated Average Cost** Cost of a service calculated to include a share of all the fixed costs and overhead costs of the organization. Such costs are divided among all of the revenue-producing activities by a formal process.

▪ **GDP or Gross Domestic Product** Sum total of all economic outputs that are produced within a country's borders.

▪ **Generalist** Nominally, any doctor who is not a specialist. Previously the term was applied to "General Practitioners" or "GPs," who had as little as one year of training after medical school. Now many "primary care" physicians are also counted as "generalists" for various purposes.

■ **Generic Drugs**   Drugs that are essentially identical to brand name drugs—without the brand name—sold by other manufacturers at lower prices than the original product.

■ **Global Budget**   Setting the total volume of expenditures in a health care system in advance.

■ **Graduate Medical Education** (sometimes Postgraduate Medical Education)   Additional training undertaken by physicians beyond medical school. The various training programs are based in hospitals and are accredited by the appropriate society for each type of study. Those in such training (i.e., residents) provide patient care under the supervision of senior physicians.

■ **Group Health Association**   A trade association of the major HMOs.

■ **Head Tax**   A tax that does not vary at all with income. Financing health care with insurance premiums is equivalent to a head tax and as such is extremely "regressive."

■ **Health Alliance**   An organization that would act as an expert buyer of health insurance for small businesses and individuals. Usually envisaged as an independent nonprofit entity, although some large employers could act as their own corporate Health Alliances.

■ **Health Insurance Association of America or HIAA**   A trade association of many for-profit health insurance companies in the United States. Many of these companies also sell other kinds of insurance.

■ **HIPC or Health Insurance Purchasing Cooperative**   See Health Alliance.

■ **HMO or Health Maintenance Organization**   An organization that provides comprehensive medical care for a fixed annual fee. HMOs vary from those that rely on salaried doctors ("staff model") to those that have a network of affiliated physicians ("IPA").

■ **Holdbacks**   Sums of money due to doctors in an HMO or other managed-care system—which are not paid until overall volume for the period can be determined. Then if volume is higher than planned, enough is permanently withheld to meet preset expenditure targets.

■ **Hospital-Based Physicians** Doctors who function as an integral part of the hospital's operation and see patients within the hospital. Radiologists, pathologists, and anesthesiologists are in this category. These specialists often have very complex financial relationships with the hospitals in which they work.

■ **House Officer or House Staff** See Residents.

■ **Iatrogenic Injury** Injuries caused by the process of health care. Not necessarily due to negligence, they could also be the result of mistaken policies, bad luck, insufficient skill, etc.

■ **Imaging Devices** Machines for creating images of the interior of the human body. Such technologies include X-ray, MRI, CAT scan, and ultrasound.

■ **Indirect Teaching Cost Adjustment** A special provision of the Medicare funding system that provides extra money to teaching hospitals for those costs which cannot be directly identified. These sums now amount to approximately $50,000 per "resident" per year.

■ **Individual Mandate** Requirement that all individuals purchase health insurance. This proposal is usually combined with an "employer mandate" and with some scheme for aiding low-income workers and the unemployed with the costs of such coverage.

■ **Industrial Red-Lining** Not selling health insurance to individuals or companies in certain sectors because they are likely to have high levels of medical expenses. A technique of "risk selection."

■ **Infant Mortality** Strictly, all deaths of infants who are born alive within the first year of their life. Thus, stillbirths do not count as infant deaths.

■ **Infectious Disease** A disease produced by the transmission of a micro-organism from one individual to another.

■ **Insurance Pool**   An analytical and financial device used by insurance companies who "pool" the loss experience of groups of subscribers (often including individuals and small business groups) to set rates that cover costs.

■ **Intensive Care**   A hospital service in which patients are attached to electronic monitors which track their vital functions as well as to other equipment that supports their breathing, etc. Large hospitals will have specialized units for heart attack victims (cardiac intensive care) and for those recovering from surgery as well as units that offer intermediate levels of intensity. Such units use four to six times as much nursing staff as ordinary medical/surgical units.

■ **IPA or Independent Practice Association**   An HMO that relies on a network of physicians practicing in their own offices who are in turn paid on a fee-for-service basis.

■ **Jackson Hole Group**   A private group of businessmen, health care executives, and academics that has developed a specific detailed plan for a "managed-competition" system.

■ **JCAHO**   (pronounced jay-co) Joint Commission on Accreditation of Healthcare Organizations. An industry self-regulatory group that sets a variety of staffing, organizational, design, and managerial standards for hospitals and other kinds of health care organizations such as nursing homes and psychiatric facilities.

■ **Job-Lock**   Inability of individuals to change jobs because they believe they will not be able to get health insurance coverage if they do change.

■ **Loss Experience**   The amount health insurance companies pay for the health care used by their policyholders.

■ **LPN/LVN Licensed Practical Nurse/Licensed Vocational Nurse**   The former term is more common in the North and East, the latter in the South and West. The designation is earned as a result of study in an accredited program in a vocational or technical school, often at the secondary level. Passing a licensing exam, noticeably less rigorous than the RN exam, is also required.

■ **Managed Care**   A system for operating a health insurance program where utilization of services is controlled by various techniques—including limiting coverage to care provided by specially selected doctors and hospitals. Such schemes also use "utilization review" or "second opinion" programs and often require "prior approval."

▪ **Managed Competition**   A health care reform plan that would foster competition among HMO-like entities that would cover all care for a fixed fee. These entities, called Accountable Health Plans, would in turn be selected by Health Alliances or HIPCs—which would purchase insurance on behalf of small companies and individuals.

▪ **Medicaid**   A joint federal and state program of health insurance for the poor and disabled, adopted in 1965. It is paid for by general tax revenue—50 to 80 percent by the federal government, depending on a state's income. About 70 percent of those covered are women and children eligible for AFDC (i.e. welfare) but the 30 percent who are disabled incur more than 70 percent of the costs.

▪ **Medical Staff**   All the physicians who are allowed to admit patients to a specific hospital. In most hospitals the existing staff decides who else may join. Most staff members derive their income from patients—they are not paid by the hospital.

▪ **Medical Underwriting**   The process of setting the price for a health insurance policy by using the actual health status of the person or group that is covered to estimate their likely future claims. The opposite of "community rating."

▪ **Medicare**   Offers hospital insurance (Part A) and coverage for doctor visits (Part B), mostly to those over sixty-five. Adopted in 1965 as part of the Social Security Act. Part A is financed by the Social Security Payroll Tax. Part B is voluntary and financed out of premiums from those who enroll and general federal tax revenue.

▪ **Medigap Insurance**   Health insurance policies purchased by individuals covered by Medicare that pay for those expenses that are not covered by Medicare.

▪ **Moral Hazard**   The possibility that insured individuals will take greater risks knowing that their losses will be covered. In health care, the idea that individuals with health insurance will take fewer steps to prevent disease.

■ **MRI or Magnetic Resonance Imaging** A sophisticated machine for making images of soft tissue (i.e., not bones). Such images now cost $600 to $700 each.

■ **National Health Board** An organization that would be created under some forms of "managed competition." The board would specify the "standard" benefit plan and oversee the functioning of the Health Alliances or HIPCs.

■ **Neighborhood Health Center** Organizations in some cities that provide ambulatory health care in poor neighborhoods. They are financed by a mixture of patient care revenues (predominantly from Medicaid) as well as various grants and subsidiaries.

■ **No Fault Malpractice Insurance** A plan for reforming malpractice law which would no longer make it necessary for injured parties to prove that their injury was the result of negligence. Instead, all persons injured by health care would be able to collect for damages. Similar plans for automobile accident insurance operate in several states.

■ **Nurse Practitioners** Individuals with special training beyond their RN preparation—typically at the master's level. They function independently although under some supervision by a physician (a very controversial boundary).

■ **Nurse's Aide** (also nursing assistant or a variety of other titles) Individuals who assist RNs and LPNs after a few months' training, usually within the hospital. In most states these personnel are not licensed.

■ **OECD** Organization of Economic Cooperation and Development. An international organization that includes all Western European nations, the United States, Canada, New Zealand, Australia, and Japan. Among other functions, the organization collects and publishes many kinds of comparative national statistics including health statistics.

■ **Open Enrollment Period** An annual period of one or more weeks during which individuals are able to switch among competing health insurance plans. Already implemented by many large employers, it would be mandatory for all Accountable Health Plans under "managed competition."

■ **Outcome Standards Management Board** A new organization that would be created under some forms of "managed competition." It would be responsible for developing measures of health care quality that would have to be publicly reported by all Accountable Health Plans.

■ **Out-of-Pocket Costs** Direct individual payments for care, including what they pay for "co-insurance" and "deductibles" as well as payments for uncovered services.

■ **Outpatient Care** Care offered by a hospital to patients who are not admitted to the hospital.

■ **Outpatient or Ambulatory Surgery** Surgery that is done on an outpatient basis. This means that the patient cannot stay overnight at the institution doing the operation. Such care is offered by hospitals or by freestanding centers.

■ **Pathology** The medical specialty devoted to the operation of clinical laboratories.

■ **Payer** (sometimes "third-party payer") Any individual or organization that pays for health care services—including insurance companies and various government programs like Medicare and Medicaid.

■ **Peer Review** The process by which government agencies that support scientific research decide on what research to support. Panels of experts in a given field review and rate proposed projects on their scientific merit.

■ **Physician Assistant** Individual who has completed a training program (inspired in part by the example of medical corpsmen during the Vietnam War). Enrollees have some prior practical experience. Individuals so trained function under the guidance and supervision of physicians.

■ **Preexisting Condition Exclusion** A provision of a health insurance plan which says that the costs of caring for an illness a subscriber already has will not be paid. The exclusion lasts for a specified period, usually one or two years.

■ **Prevention** Refers to all efforts to prevent disease from developing—from efforts aimed at encouraging better nutrition and exercise to attempts to diminish drunk driving and teen violence or to improve air pollution.

■ **Primary Care** Medical practice based on direct contact with the patient without referral from another physician. Such practice is undertaken by doctors trained in various ways including pediatricians, obstetricians, general internists, family physicians, and general practitioners. In addition, many specialists in fact engage in a significant amount of primary care.

■ **Primary Prevention** Refers to efforts by the health care system to prevent or cure disease before it has occurred. Screening for as-yet-undetected disease (e.g., mammography for breast cancer) is considered primary prevention.

■ **Prior Approval** A form of "utilization review" where an insurance company requires a hospital or doctor to get permission from the insurance company before providing care.

■ **Private Insurance** Any health insurance policy that is not government financed. It also includes the policies that cover government workers.

■ **Profile Monitoring** A process in which the practice patterns of individual physicians are compared to various norms. The purpose is to identify those who use surgery, tests, or hospitalization especially frequently. Already done by some insurance companies, independent agencies, and by the medical societies in each state in Germany.

■ **Proprietary (for-profit) Hospital** A hospital operated as a normal corporation. Most such hospitals are part of large chains.

■ **Protocol** A guide for the treatment of a given disease or condition. Often the protocol has conditional instructions of the form "if this happens . . . do that."

■ **Provider** Any individual or organization that provides health care services. Thus, mainly doctors and hospitals but also dentists, nursing homes, home care agencies, etc.

▪ **Public Good** An economics concept that refers to a good (or service) that affects more than one individual at a time—like air pollution or national defense. The opposite idea is a private (or ordinary) good that benefits only the purchaser.

▪ **Public Health** Refers to a wide variety of activities directed mainly at disease prevention, although also concerned with the organization of health care services. Most cities and states have departments of public health and some universities have schools to train students (often physicians) for such roles.

▪ **Rationing** Process of limiting the use of all possible health care services. Rationing can be done by price, by waiting lists, or by deciding not to provide certain services.

▪ **RBRVS or Resource Based Relative Value Scale** A system for paying doctors instituted by Medicare. Each type of encounter or treatment is assigned a "relative value"—typically a number of points—based on the time, skill, and training required of the doctor. Then the entire fee structure can be adjusted up or down by setting the payment for each point. Similar schemes are used in Germany, Canada, and Japan.

▪ **Residents** (also called "house officers" or "house staff") Individuals who have graduated from medical school (and thus are called "doctor") who have not yet completed their training. Typically, residents work in teaching hospitals from one to six years—depending on the specialty—receiving what is called "graduate medical education."

▪ **Risk Adjustment** Paying an insurance company or Accountable Health Plan extra for enrolling subscribers who have higher than average health care costs.

▪ **Risk Management** Process by which a hospital or HMO limits its risk for being sued for malpractice, sometimes also used as a synonym for "risk selection."

▪ **Risk Selection** Process by which an insurer limits the "risks" it will cover. In health insurance, the process of encouraging sicker individuals not to enroll in your health insurance plan.

▪ **RN or Registered Nurse** A professional title earned by passing an examination supervised by a state board of nursing, after completing the required education. In most states certain specific nursing tasks must be performed by RNs.

■ **Roemer's Law**   Named for Milton Roemer, it states "A bed built is a bed filled." More generally it summarizes the observation that added capacity can lead to added health care utilization.

■ **Rural Health Centers**   Health care organizations in rural areas designed to provide comprehensive "outpatient services." They typically employ several physicians plus other kinds of health care workers. They are financed by patient revenues plus various kinds of grant programs.

■ **Secondary Prevention**   Efforts made by the health care system to prevent disease—or its recurrence—once a patient has an illness.

■ **Self-Insure**   A health insurance strategy in which a large employer or employee group acts as its own insurance company, collecting premiums and paying claims out of what is collected. Groups that do this also purchase "reinsurance" against the risk of an unanticipated combination of large claims in a single year.

■ **Single-Payer**   A health care reform plan that would create a single government health insurance organization that would cover everyone. Care would be provided by existing doctors and hospitals, operating independently but paid by the single-payer.

■ **Specialist**   Strictly, any physician who has pursued specialty training beyond the first year of residency. More loosely, those specialists who do not provide "primary care."

■ **Specialty Societies**   Medical societies in each of the major areas of medical practice. They regulate and accredit residency programs in their area of competence and establish the requirements and operate the process for becoming board-certified in their respective specialties.

■ **Spend Down**   A requirement under many state Medicaid programs that individuals use up their assets when these are above the level required for eligibility before being able to collect benefits.

■ **SSI or Supplemental Security Income**   A federal program of income support for those who are disabled. Disability covers many conditions including mental illness, mental retardation, and infectious disease. Thus, some of those infected with AIDS are covered by SSI, which in turn makes them eligible for Medicaid.

■ **Standard Benefit Package** Minimum coverage offered by all Accountable Health Plans in a "managed-competition" system.

■ **Subspecialist** Strictly, any physician who has gone on to specialized training beyond the training for general surgery, general internal medicine, or pediatrics. Within internal medicine, for example, there are many subspecialties such as those in oncology (cancer), nephrology (kidney disease), or cardiology (heart disease).

■ **Teaching Hospital** Strictly, any hospital that has any residency program. Since many hospitals have one or two such programs, the distinction is often made as to which are major teaching hospitals, i.e., those that have a significant teaching role.

■ **Tort Reform** Refers to a variety of proposals to reform malpractice law in particular and more generally the law on all liability for injuries (which is called tort law). These proposals include simplified procedures, limits on awards, limits on attorneys' fees, and, more radically, "no fault" schemes or "enterprise liability."

■ **Underwriting** Process by which an insurance company decides how much to charge for an insurance policy. Generally based on how much the company expects to have to pay out for claims under the policy.

■ **Utilization Review** A process by which an insurance company reviews decisions by doctors and hospitals on what care to provide for patients. Often focused on how long patients stay in hospitals.

■ **Volume Performance Standards** These state the volume of physician services that the managers of a health plan expect to be provided in a given period.

ACKNOWLEDGMENTS AND NOTES ON SOURCES

In a book designed for the general reader, we have chosen not to follow the scholarly convention of footnoting each and every reference. However, it does seem appropriate to indicate the main sources we have drawn upon—as well as to acknowledge the aid and assistance, over the years, of some especially helpful individuals.

Much of the work on hospital organization draws on a large number of hospital site visits conducted in connection with several distinct projects supported by the Commonwealth Fund of New York. The aid, encouragement, and substantive advice of three individuals from the Fund—Margaret Mahoney, President; Tom Maloney, formerly Senior Vice President; and Mo Katz, Senior Program Officer—have been invaluable. Colleagues from those projects have played a major role in informing various parts of the analysis of this volume. Particularly helpful over the years have been Ann Minnick of Rush Presbyterian Hospital in Chicago; Thomas Delbanco, Susan Edgeman-Levitan, and Paul Cleary of the Picker Commonwealth Patient Centered Care Project in Boston; and Alice Chapin and David Soule of the Maine Health Information Center.

Several colleagues from the Harvard School of Public Health have also been extremely helpful, including Robert Blendon, whose work on public opinion in health care reform informed Chapter 1; Harvey Fineberg, Dean of the School, whose work on medical technology influenced the argument in Chapter 2; William Hsiao, whose work on insurance company behavior and

179

reimbursement systems was very helpful in Chapter 3; and Nancy Kane, whose work on hospital accounting and finance also had a major impact on Chapter 3.

In constructing and interpreting the international comparative analysis, we have been greatly aided by Professors Michael Arnold and Konrad Selbmann of the University of Tubingen in Germany, as well as by Christian Koeck of the Vienna Municipal Hospital System and Ian Wronski of the University of Nor' Queensland in Australia. Harald Jodalen helped us gather dat from Norway. Karl Lauterbach was also helpful with the Euro- pean work, as well as being a major source of ideas on the underlying ethical issues. Many other colleagues, students, public officials, and health care managers—really far too numerous for us to mention them all—have also been generous with their time, insights, and advice over the years. None of these individuals— mentioned or unmentioned—bear any responsibility for the con- clusions we have advanced or the uses, or misuses, we have made of their work.

As for specific sources, for Chapter 1 see Blendon, R. J., et al., *The Future of American Healthcare,* Volumes I and II, Faulk- ner and Gray, 1993. See also Levit, et al., "Americans' Health Insurance Coverage, 1980–1991," in the Fall 1992 issue of *Health Care Financing Review,* as well as Blendon, R. J., et al., in *Journal of the American Medical Association,* December 16, 1992, and Sullivan, C. B., et al., in *Health Affairs,* Winter 1992.

For Chapter 2, see Jack Wennberg's work on small area variations in *Scientific American* in 1982. Also important are Robert H. Brook's many papers on appropriateness. See for example Winslow et. al., "The Appropriateness of Carotid End- arterectomy," *New England Journal of Medicine,* March 24, 1988, and also Brook and Leape's work on CABG in the February 10, 1993, issue of the *Journal of the American Medical Association.* Chapter 2 also presents data from *Health United States, 1991,* published by the U.S. Department of Health and Human Services.

For Chapter 3, see Sylvia Law, *Blue Cross: What Went Wrong,* Yale University Press, 1974. Nancy Kane's work was extensively reported in the *Boston Globe,* May 9, 1993. See also Stevens, R., *In Sickness and in Wealth: American Hospitals in the Twentieth Century,* Basic Books, Inc., 1989; Berwick, D. M., et al., *Curing Health Care: New Strategies for Quality Improvement,* Jossey-Bass, 1991; Shortell et al., *Strategic Choices for America's Hospitals: Managing Change in Turbulent Times,* Jossey-Bass, 1991; and Fein, R., *Medical Care, Medical Costs: The Search for a Health Insurance Policy,* Harvard University Press, 1989.

Chapter 4 presents 1991 OECD data published by George Schieber, Jean Pierre Poullier, and Leslie Greenwald in the Summer 1993 issue of *Health Affairs.* A variety of technical sources were also helpful here, including pieces by the following authors in the indicated journals: Fuchs, V. R., *Journal of the American Medical Association,* February 3, 1993; Ginzberg, E., et al., *Journal of the American Medical Association,* May 15, 1991; Grogan, C. M., *Journal of Health Politics, Policy and Law,* Summer 1992; Grumbach, K., et al., *New England Journal of Medicine,* April 1, 1993; Holahan, J. et al., *Inquiry,* Summer 1992; Kirkman-Liff, B. L., *Journal of the American Medical Association,* May 15, 1991; J. Newhouse, *Health Affairs,* Supplement 1993; Reinhardt, U. E., *Health Affairs,* 1993 Supplement issue; Thorpe, K. E., *Health Affairs,* Summer 1992; Wicks, E. K., *German Health Care: Financing, Administration and Coverage,* Health Insurance Association of America, 1992; Evans, R. G., *Strained Mercy: The Economics of Canadian Health Care,* Butterworths (Toronto), 1984.

Chapter 4 also relies on work by Phil Caper and John Billings, who coined the term "Ambulatory Care Sensitive Condition." Their latest works are in the Summer 1993 issue of *Health Affairs.*

Alain Enthoven has written extensively about his managed competition proposal, most recently in the 1993 Supplement issue of *Health Affairs,* which is devoted to articles on managed competition. His analysis of the FEHBP appeared in the Fall 1989 issue of *Health Affairs.*

Joe Newhouse's work on risk selection and HMO costs can be found in the 1982 *Journal of Health Economics,* and while his analysis on the costs of HMOs appears in the August 1985 issue of *Medical Care,* Paul Starr, Walter Zelman, Stuart Altman, Alan Cohen, Henry Aaron, and Bill Schwartz all argue in the 1993

Supplement issue of *Health Affairs* for the need for a national expenditure budget. On technical matters, see Blendon, R. J., et al., in *Journal of the American Medical Association*, May 13, 1992; Hellinger, F. J., *Health Care Financing Review*, Winter 1987; Kronick, R., et al., *New England Journal of Medicine*, January 14, 1993; Langwell, K. M., et al., *Health Care Financing Review*, Winter 1989; and Price, J. R., et al., *Journal of Health Economics*, 1983.

Steffie Woolhandler and David Himmelstein have written much of the important work on the Canadian system. Most recently, with Kevin Grumbach, they described the advantages of such a system in the May 15, 1991, issue of the *Journal of the American Medical Association*.

Chapter 6 summarizes the findings reported in *A Measure of Malpractice*, written by P. C. Weiler et al., Harvard University Press, 1993. People interested in mental health care should consult the Fall 1992 issue of *Health Affairs*. Steve Schroeder and Lewis Sandy wrote on the specialty distribution of U.S. physicians in the April 1, 1993, issue of the *New England Journal of Medicine*.

MJR
ATC
Boston, Mass.
September 1993